JAMESTOWN  PUBLISHERS

FRIGHT WRITE

Your Worst Nightmare

FrightWrite

An ESSENTIALLY EERIE Reading and Writing Program

Your Worst Nightmare

JAMESTOWN PUBLISHERS
A DIVISION OF NTC/CONTEMPORARY
PUBLISHING COMPANY

Manufactured in the United States of America.
International Standard Book Number: 0-89061-862-3
10 9 8 7 6 5 4 3 2 1

Executive Editor
Marilyn Cunningham

Project Editor
Gretchen Kalinoski

Production and Design
PiperStudiosInc

Cover Composition
Doug Besser

CONTENTS

To the Reader

READ AT YOUR OWN RISK

What are you afraid of? Come on, read this book—we dare you. After all, what's the worst that could happen? Yes, the stories will give you the creeps. Sure, you'll probably become afraid of the dark. Oh, you may have trouble falling asleep, too. But what are you afraid of?

Amazingly, the stories in this book can also help you overcome a big fear many students have—a fear of writing! See how professional writers get their story ideas and create convincing characters. Find out how to paint ghastly pictures in the minds of your readers and create an eerie mood. Learn how to tell a story that will give your audience nightmares. Learn how to **FRIGHTWRITE!**

SHADOWS OF DOUBT

Everyone is afraid of something. That's what we're counting on!

In the blink of an eye you might suddenly feel

That your world's been invaded by all things unreal.

They slink up behind you and don't make a sound,

But there's nothing to fear . . . if you don't turn around.

In the pit of your stomach there rests a device

That calculates how fast your blood turns to ice;

It measures the temperature nightmares will start,

Then divides it by beats of a terrified heart.

At the foot of your bed lies a blanket of fear,

You might think it's quite safe, but it's always quite near.

When its steel-woolen quilting wraps 'round you one night,

You may learn that it's not only bedbugs that bite.

At the top of the stairs there's an attic I've found,

That remained even after the house was torn down,

And it's filled with the cobwebs of lonely old dreams,

Which have grown into nightmares that swing from the beams.

At the mouth of a cave lives a shadow of doubt,

If you dare to go in, will you ever come out?

Are there creatures who lurk where it's too dim to see?

Can you hear when they move? Are you scared yet? (Who, me?)

At the edge of the earth flows a river of fear,

And it pours into space day by day, year by year.

As you shoot the cold rapids and stray far from shore,

Do you notice your lifeboat has just lost an oar?

In the eye of the storm stands a ghost of a chance,

And around her all spirits are destined to dance.

She turns a cold gaze toward an unlucky few—

Don't dare to look now, for she's staring at you.

At the end of the world stands a giant steel door,

And what lies beyond it, nobody's quite sure . . .

Is it crystal-clear heavens or night blazing hot,

And which is more frightening: knowing or not?

In the face of the future we fly on our own,

Hoping our wings never turn into stone.

If you fall from that sky to the sea, will you drown?

Well, there's no need to worry . . . unless you look down.

At the back of your mind, there's a hole open wide,

Where the darkness is creeping in from the outside,

You can light rows of candles to cast the dark out,

But it's always there hiding . . .

> . . . in shadows of doubt.

THE DRESSING ROOM

Until today, Sarah Jane Rogers's biggest fear was that she'd never have a boyfriend. Little does she know that will be the least of her worries.

Y ou're not going out dressed like that, are you?" Her mother's voice stopped Sarah Jane Rogers at the front door.

She sighed loudly and rolled her eyes. "What's wrong with how I'm dressed?"

Sarah Jane's mother looked disapprovingly at her fourteen-year-old daughter, dressed in tattered maroon leggings, a shapeless cotton dress, and a man's brown sweater frayed at the cuffs. "You look," Mrs. Rogers said, "like a bag lady."

"Oh, please!" Sarah Jane moaned and opened the door.

But her mother's voice stopped her again. "And where did you get those boots?"

Sarah Jane looked at her feet. Okay, so maybe the boots were a size too big, but Terese and Angel, her new best friends, had told her just to wear an extra pair of socks. "I got them last week at the surplus store," she said impatiently. "I told you. Don't you remember?"

"You mean that old warehouse on River Road?" Again her mother frowned. "But it's so . . . dirty. And trucks

surplus store: a store that sells clothing and other items that didn't sell at other stores

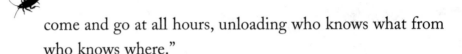

come and go at all hours, unloading who knows what from who knows where."

Sarah Jane shrugged. "But they've got the coolest clothes." She proudly lifted the skirt of her cotton dress to show off her new leggings. "Can you believe I only paid fifty cents for these?"

Sarah Jane's mother sucked in her breath. "But, honey, somebody else has worn those stockings."

"I know. So?"

"So? So they aren't clean! I want you to take them off and throw them away."

"Mom!" Sarah Jane yelped.

"I'll give you some money and you can go shopping at a real store," her mother insisted.

"But I like *these* clothes," Sarah Jane said. "Terese says they make me look mysterious."

Mrs. Rogers raised an eyebrow. "Who's Terese?"

"She's my new friend. She and Angel are going to be fashion designers."

"I suppose they're the ones who talked you into buying those ridiculous clothes." She shook her head. "Sarah Jane, you are so <u>gullible</u>."

"My clothes are *not* ridiculous!"

Mrs. Rogers sighed. "Oh, honey, when are you going to learn to think for yourself?"

Sarah Jane began to tap the toe of her oversized boot. "Can I go now?"

gullible: easily fooled or cheated

"No," her mother said firmly. "I know nothing about these new friends of yours, but I *do* know I don't want you in that filthy warehouse again."

"But I told Terese and Angel I'd meet them at the surplus store at one o'clock."

"You're not going, and that's final," her mother said, walking away.

As Sarah Jane slumped down on the bottom stair step, she caught sight of herself in the hall mirror. She stood up and turned this way and that, checking out her appearance. She was short and round, and clothes couldn't change that. She had to admit that maybe the sweater did look shabby. But Terese had told her the layers of clothes would hide the extra pounds Sarah Jane just couldn't seem to shed.

Sarah Jane looked at the front door. She was tempted to meet her friends anyway. For three weeks in a row, she had met Terese and Angel at the warehouse. She enjoyed the attention they gave her, pulling clothes off the metal racks for her to try on in the dressing room. Before she had begun hanging around with them, Sarah Jane thought, she'd been very plain. But the clothes her new friends picked out for her had changed all that. She was starting to feel good about herself, starting to think that maybe one day she could actually attract a boyfriend.

If you were Sarah Jane, what would you do?

Sarah Jane heard her mother talking on the kitchen phone. Mrs. Rogers ran a catering business, and Sarah Jane knew she would be busy all afternoon. After a moment's hesitation and pushing away the last hint of guilt, she slipped quietly out the door.

✳ ✳ ✳

At the surplus store, a tractor trailer was backed up to the loading dock. Two men were dragging huge rolls of carpets that looked like fat pillars from the truck. As Sarah Jane stepped over the carpets piled in front of the warehouse door, one of the men unloading the truck called out, "Hey, kid!"

At first, Sarah Jane didn't realize he meant her. "Me?" she asked, stopping short. She thought he wasn't going to let her go inside the warehouse.

The man grinned, showing a mouth full of rotted teeth. "You want to buy a carpet?"

Sarah Jane shook her head no and turned away.

"Wait!" he said. "They're not just carpets, they're beautiful rugs." He knelt down and pulled back a corner of one of the rolled carpets to reveal a colorful floral pattern. "Good quality," he said, smoothing his fingers over the pile.

Sarah Jane smiled politely, but then she squealed and covered her mouth with her hand as three large black bugs scurried from inside the rolls of the rug. Two of them disappeared between the cracks in the loading platform. But the third was not as lucky. The rug man snatched it up between his dirty fingers.

"Cockroach," he said, then laughed at Sarah Jane's disgust. He held the bug up close to his bearded face. Its long black antennae waved frantically in the air.

"*Eeeuw!*" Sarah Jane cried, then laughed at her fear. For one terrifying moment, Sarah Jane thought he was going to throw the bug at her.

"Imported," the man said, grinning, "all the way from Asia." He laughed loudly again. Then, as Sarah Jane stared in disbelief, he closed his hand around the roach and ate it.

"*Eeeuw!*" she cried louder and hurried into the warehouse. She could still hear the rug man laughing.

Then she heard the thump of another rolled carpet dropping from the truck to the platform floor.

She found Terese and Angel in the basement, browsing through the clothes racks. When Sarah Jane told them what had happened on the loading platform, they didn't believe her. "He was just teasing you," Angel said. "Don't you know when someone is teasing you?"

Sarah Jane shivered. "Okay, so maybe he didn't actually eat the cockroach, but it sure looked like it." She stared at the wooden planks of the warehouse floor. "There are probably roaches all over this place," she said.

Terese shrugged. "So what if there are? Cockroaches don't bite."

"No, but they multiply really fast," Angel said. She leaned close to Sarah Jane. "They lay their eggs in the glue of cardboard boxes and in the cracks in wood."

"They do not!" Sarah Jane said. "Do they?"

"Sure."

"How do you know?" Sarah Jane asked.

"I did a research paper on them last year," Angel said. "Did you know cockroaches have been around since the Ice Age? Nothing kills them. And they can fly, too."

"You're just making that up," Sarah Jane said. "Cockroaches only come out at night. They're afraid of the light." She glanced nervously around the dimly lit warehouse, wishing suddenly that it had more lights, like the bright spotlights in the stores at the mall.

"The kind from Asia have wings," Angel said. "They can fly right into your mouth and down your throat and choke you!"

Notice how the author provides you with gruesome facts about cockroaches—adding to your own fears!

"Stop it!" Sarah Jane said sharply.

Angel and Terese burst into laughter. "You are so gullible," Terese said. "You'll believe anything!"

Sarah Jane realized now that they were teasing her. She smiled weakly.

"You're not going to get mad at us now, are you, Sarah Jane?" asked Angel.

Sarah Jane picked at the frayed sleeve of her old brown sweater. "No," she said quietly. Then she added, "But I don't like being called gullible."

"But that's why we like you," Angel said. "Because you are gullible. You're so innocent all the time."

"I am?"

"Sure. That's why you always make us laugh," Terese said, walking over to another rack of clothes with Angel right behind her.

Sarah Jane followed the girls, realizing that the warehouse was nearly empty. In fact, only two other people were shopping. A strong musty odor seemed to be rising from the old clothes on the hangers. Sarah Jane had never noticed the smell before. Her mother was right—the place

really *was* dirty. Still, Sarah Jane felt drawn to Angel and Terese, and after a moment, she followed them toward the back of the warehouse basement.

"Whoa!" Terese pulled a yellow <u>tunic</u> from the clothes rack. "Look at this!" The tunic had fringe around the neck, with colorful glass beads, like tiny marbles, tied to the ends of the fringe. "Three dollars!" The marblelike beads clinked as Terese held the tunic up to her neck and turned to Sarah Jane. "How does it look?"

tunic: a long shirt that extends below the waist

Sarah Jane shrugged. "Okay, I guess." She glanced at the floor around her feet. She was glad she was wearing boots. If she saw another roach, she'd stomp it good. Then she remembered how quickly the roaches had scurried from the rolled-up rug and disappeared into the cracks in the floor. A roach could run right up her leg before she even knew it. Just thinking about it made her skin crawl.

"I think it would look better on Sarah Jane," Angel said.

"Me, too," Terese said. She held out the tunic to Sarah Jane. "Go ahead. Try it on."

Sarah Jane looked up. "Huh? Oh, I don't want it. You can have it."

"But don't you like it, Sarah Jane? I think it would be perfect for you. You know, hide some of that extra tummy you have." She patted her own flat stomach and grinned.

Sarah Jane blushed. Both Terese and Angel were tall and skinny. The clothes they wore didn't have to hide anything. "I don't know," Sarah Jane began. "I don't—"

"Just try it on," Terese urged. "You'll never know how it will look until you try it on."

"But I don't want to try it on," Sarah Jane insisted.

"Why not?" Terese asked.

Sarah Jane didn't answer right away. "My . . . my mother says these clothes are dirty," she finally admitted.

"So, you can clean it when you get it home," Angel said matter-of-factly. "That's what we do."

"My mother also thinks the clothes I get here look ridiculous," Sarah Jane added.

"Is that what she told you?" Terese asked.

Sarah Jane nodded.

Should Sarah Jane try on the tunic? Would you? Why or why not?

"Well, who are you going to listen to—your mother or us?" Terese asked, her arms folded across her chest.

Sarah Jane wasn't sure.

"Doesn't your mother know you're old enough to pick out your own clothes now?" Angel asked, tapping her foot impatiently. "Go ahead!" Angel said, shoving Sarah Jane firmly toward the dressing room door. "Try it on, and we'll wait for you out here."

Reluctantly, Sarah Jane took the tunic and opened the door. She peered inside. The room was lit with a dusty, naked light bulb. Sarah Jane saw nothing scurrying over the floor, so she stepped inside. She closed the heavy door and locked it with the bolt.

For a moment, she was glad to be away from Angel and Terese. Something seemed different about them today. They had never teased her and laughed at her before. Still wearing her dress, leggings, and ratty sweater, she stared at her reflection in the mirror. Terese and Angel had said these clothes looked great on her, and she had believed them. But now, in the bright light of the dressing room, Sarah Jane wasn't so sure anymore. Sure, other kids wore grungy clothes. On them, they looked cool. But what Sarah Jane saw now was that the clothes didn't make her look thinner at all. If anything, she looked even heavier.

She held the tunic up in front of her. The glass beads tinkled. She really didn't like it, she decided. And anyway, her mother would never let her wear it to school.

"Do you have it on yet?" Angel asked from the other side of the door.

Sarah Jane bit her lip. She felt all confused. She didn't like the tunic, but she didn't want to make Angel and Terese mad. *Oh well*, she thought, *I can at least try it on and show them. I don't have to buy it.*

She pulled off her sweater and dropped it on the floor. Suddenly, there was a loud thump overhead. Startled, Sarah Jane looked up at the ceiling. She heard a second thump and realized that the dressing room was directly below the loading platform. As a third heavy object hit the floor, a fine cloud of sawdust slipped through the cracks in the ceiling.

"Sarah Jane?" Angel called. "We're going upstairs to look at the jewelry. Come up when you're finished."

"Wait!" Sarah Jane called to them, feeling oddly panicked about being left alone down in the basement of the warehouse. "I'm finished now. The tunic doesn't fit."

"Don't hurry!" Terese called back. "Take your time."

"Wait!" Sarah Jane called again, her weird feeling of fear increasing. *But why?*

Then she heard a sound like paper crinkling . . . from above. Slowly, she glanced up and saw a huge cockroach on the ceiling. She screamed, dropping the tunic, and backed against the wall. Another roach crawled from between the cracks in the ceiling, waving its antennae as if it were looking at her. Then it unfolded its wings and fluttered.

"Oh, no!" Sarah Jane breathed. She turned and fumbled with the bolt on the door, but it was jammed. "Angel! Terese!" she shouted. "Don't leave me. I'm locked in here."

There was no answer. Sarah Jane pounded on the heavy door. "Somebody, help! I'm stuck in here! Get me out!"

She felt something flick against her cheek, and she swept her hand across her face. A cockroach fell to the floor. She tried to stomp it with her heavy boot, but she wasn't quick enough and it scurried away into the corner.

Again Sarah Jane struggled with the bolt. No matter how she pulled and pushed on it, it wouldn't budge. Above her, another roll of carpeting thumped on the loading platform. Three . . . six . . . eight cockroaches crawled through the cracks and spread their wings. "Stop!" Sarah Jane shouted at the ceiling. "Stop unloading the carpets!" But no one seemed to hear.

She began to kick at the door. "Angel! Terese!" she shouted frantically. The roaches were flying all around her now. There were a thousand little ticking sounds as the creatures' wings flopped open and closed. Roaches were crawling all over the mirror, all over her sweater in the middle of the floor, all over . . . *everything*!

Is Sarah Jane behaving rationally? Or has fear set in?

Suddenly, one of the horrible insects flew into her hair. Shrieking, Sarah Jane swatted at it. She tried to stomp on the roaches scuttling around her feet, but the bugs seemed indestructible. They appeared dead, but then scurried back to life again.

Thump! Another rug hit the ceiling above the bug-infested dressing room.

More roaches squeezed through the cracks above Sarah Jane. She huddled against the door, her arms over her head. "Someone, please," she whimpered. "Open the door. I want to go home."

Thump. Thump. Rug after rug hit the ceiling, and bug after bug appeared right after. There seemed to be a

million roaches in the dressing room now, crawling, flying, running up Sarah Jane's legs and flicking against her hair, her cheeks, and her lips.

Sarah Jane began to cry. "Stop it!" she wailed, and as she did, a cockroach flew into her mouth. She gagged and sputtered, unable to breathe.

Thump. Thump. Thump. The carpets striking the ceiling were like a heartbeat. Then the thumping stopped. The only sound in the dressing room was the soft scurrying of insects disappearing into the dark crevices of the wood.

Upstairs, Terese and Angel saw the large tractor trailers pulling away. The girls exchanged silent, <u>conspiratorial</u> smiles as they walked out of the warehouse.

* * *

The next Saturday at one o'clock, Terese and Angel met their new friend, Sheila, on the loading platform of the surplus store. The three girls hurried inside. "Isn't this place great?" Angel said, pulling clothes from the racks. "You just never know what you're going to find. Every week, it's something different."

"Whoa!" Terese said, holding up a green sweater with silver sequins on the front. She turned to Sheila. "Now this would really look terrific on you!"

"You think so?" Sheila asked uncertainly.

"Sure!" Angel said. "Why don't you try it on? I'll show you a dressing room. You'll never know until you try it on."

conspiratorial: in a way that suggests a secret plot against someone

THE DRESSING ROOM

▼ Learning from the Story

It's a safe bet that Catherine Gourley, the author of "The Dressing Room," is afraid of cockroaches. How else would she know exactly how to make your flesh crawl? Work with a group of two or three classmates. Make a list of all the things you're afraid of. Include things you were afraid of as a child but aren't afraid of now. Share ideas about how you might turn these fears into a truly nightmarish story.

▼ Putting It into Practice

Try one of these ideas to help you start thinking about your story.

- Take photos or draw pictures of some things that give you nightmares.
- Have someone take a photo of you facing your worst fear.
- Draw a picture of yourself reacting to something you're afraid of. What's the expression on your face? How are you behaving? What will make the fear go away?

Hang your photo or drawing up for inspiration as you turn your worst fear into a nightmarish story.

SOMETIMES TELLING THE TRUTH CAN GET YOU

HERESY

INTO MORE TROUBLE THAN TELLING A LIE.

J udge Nathaniel Gravestone slammed his <u>gavel</u>. "Bring in the accused!" he ordered.

Everyone in the small, makeshift courtroom turned to the doors located along the back wall. After a few moments, two officers in dark, seventeenth-century clothing appeared and marched their prisoner up the center aisle.

Unlike the thieves, pickpockets, and brawlers who had been brought before Judge Gravestone earlier in the day, this prisoner didn't look at all like someone who would run afoul of the law. She was a girl—by the looks of her, no more than thirteen years old—dressed in the pale, simple clothing typical of the Puritans who had settled in this part of the New World since the *Mayflower's* arrival at Plymouth approximately twenty years before. Clearly frightened, the girl kept her large brown eyes cast downward as she was led up to the front of the courtroom and directed to stand on a small wooden platform.

heresy: a belief that is different from that of people at a particular time

gavel: a large wooden mallet or hammer used to get people's attention

In the gallery, those townspeople who had come to watch the trial shifted nervously in their chairs and exchanged excited whispers. Many onlookers wore expressions of fear or hatred, as if this seemingly harmless maiden carried some wretched disease that could destroy them all.

"Charity Stamford," the judge intoned, looking down at his notes but directing his words toward the girl standing not ten feet away. "You have been accused by the good people of this village of practicing supernatural arts and engaging in other activities in violation of the laws of nature. Tell me, young lady, how do you plead?"

"Leave my child alone!" a woman cried from the courtroom gallery. This was Charity's mother, known in town as The Widow Stamford since her husband had reportedly died during the crossing from England the previous year. A thin, plain-featured woman in her early thirties, her dry, furrowed skin was marked by a lifetime of hard work and stern discipline. "My little girl is innocent! The charges are untrue!"

"Silence!" Judge Gravestone ordered, hammering his gavel on the bench before him. "This court will determine what is true and what is not!" Collecting himself, he turned back to the accused. "Now, Miss Stamford, as to the charge of engaging in the supernatural, how do you plead?"

"Not guilty," Charity replied, her dark brown eyes still downcast, her voice barely a whisper.

"You will have to speak much louder, girl," the stern magistrate instructed.

"Not guilty," Charity stated for all to hear.

gallery: a platform or balcony where people sit to watch and listen

intoned: spoke in a flat or sing-song way

magistrate: a judge

"Very well, child," Judge Gravestone grumbled, seemingly unconvinced. He turned to a tall, long-haired young man wearing the uniform of a court <u>prosecutor</u>. "Mr. Bainbridge, you may call your first witness."

Rising, Mr. Bainbridge straightened his black coat, then shouted as if wishing to be heard all the way back to England, "The People call Miss Hope Duckworth to the stand!"

For the past six years, Miss Duckworth had served as the one and only teacher at the small, one-room school in which all the children of this Pilgrim village were educated. A prim, prune-faced woman whose thin, gray hair was pulled tightly back, she marched eagerly to the witness box where she was sworn to tell the truth and nothing but.

◆————————————————◆

"MY LITTLE GIRL IS INNOCENT! THE CHARGES ARE UNTRUE!"

◆————————————————◆

"Now, Miss Duckworth, you are one of those good citizens who have accused Charity Stamford of being a <u>sorceress</u>," Mr. Bainbridge began, posing proudly before the judge. "Please tell this court what the <u>defendant</u> did to lead you to this conclusion."

"I was teaching English grammar and composition to my middle-schoolers," Miss Duckworth replied, her posture as straight as the ruler she regularly wielded against her most unruly students. "And as a writing exercise, I asked the students to construct an essay in

prosecutor: the lawyer representing the government's side of the case

sorceress: a witch

defendant: the person accused of doing something wrong

which they were to describe what life might be like here in the Massachusetts Bay Colony three hundred years hence."

"Naturally, you expected an essay imagining a society devoted to prayer, study, and the doing of charitable works," the prosecutor suggested.

"Of course," the teacher said. "With the proper spelling and punctuation, of course."

"Of course," Mr. Bainbridge said, now turning his gaze toward Charity Stamford, who shivered as she clutched the wooden railing before her. "And was this what the defendant wrote?"

"No, sir, it was not," Miss Duckworth reported. "The things she wrote about—well, I hardly dare speak of them in mixed company!"

"This is a court of law, Miss Duckworth," Judge Gravestone reminded the teacher. "You are compelled to relate the facts as you know them."

Miss Duckworth twisted her wrinkled lips as if tasting something foul, then spoke rapidly. "She wrote of a time when this village would be home to not only Englishmen, but also to Indians, Africans, Spanish, and even Chinese, all living as equal individuals in the same community."

The townsfolk in the gallery recoiled in terror.

"Go on," Mr. Bainbridge prompted.

"She wrote of men and women traveling the streets in horseless carriages, of winged ships flying through the air like birds, and of people speaking directly to one another over vast distances by holding objects to their ears and mouths," Miss Duckworth went on, eyeing Charity sternly. "Either the girl is just headstrong or she's simply speaking—"

"Heresy!" one of the townspeople shouted.

"Sorceress!" another cried.

"Off with her head!" a third demanded.

"Did you ask Charity where she got such outrageous notions?" Mr. Bainbridge inquired.

"Of course," Miss Duckworth replied haughtily. "She claimed she had a vision."

Where do you think Charity really got those outrageous ideas?

"THE THINGS SHE WROTE ABOUT—
WELL, I HARDLY DARE SPEAK
OF THEM IN MIXED COMPANY!"

Now virtually everyone in the gallery was standing, screaming for Charity Stamford's death. In the center of the near-riot, Charity's mother sat sobbing into a coarse linen handkerchief. Twenty feet away, Charity <u>cowered</u> as several spectators hurled chunks of rotted fruit and vegetables her way.

"Order!" Judge Gravestone shouted, slamming his gavel repeatedly. "I will have order in this courtroom this very instant!"

Slowly, the angry mob quieted down and returned to their seats. Standing by the witness box, Mr. Bainbridge smoothed the folds of his dark coat, then directed Miss Duckworth back to her seat.

"Thank you, Miss Duckworth," he said formally. "I have no further questions."

Mr. Bainbridge's next witness was William Franklin Hooke, a classmate of young Charity's. After putting the

cowered: drew back in fear

trembling boy under oath, Bainbridge had the handsome fourteen-year-old recount a dream the girl had related to him just a few weeks earlier. Initially reluctant to testify against his friend, William nonetheless described Charity's dream as best he could remember it.

"She said that in her dream, we no longer lived under the Crown of England. She claimed we were a free people unto ourselves," William reported, his head bowed shamefully.

"Traitor!" several men cried from the gallery.

"String her up!" another demanded.

"She said that the people of this land were free to speak as they so desired, worship as they please, and write and read without official censors," young William went on.

"Blasphemy!" shouted a bearded man.

"Hang her!" cried a round-faced woman.

"And did she say that this was, after all, only a dream?" Mr. Bainbridge inquired.

William hesitated a long moment, threw Charity a look as if to ask her forgiveness, then turned to face the humorless prosecutor. "No, sir," he replied nervously. "Charity said she believed this is the way our land will be someday."

A moment later, the courtroom erupted into chaos. It took everything the officers could do to bring the angry citizens under control. One particularly angry farmer even managed to grab hold of Charity's arm before a guard got the man in a headlock and wrestled him away.

"One more outburst like that, and I shall see you all in the stockade!" Judge Gravestone roared as the other officers slowly got the room back under control. He cleared his

blasphemy: speaking against God or other sacred things

stockade: a pen where prisoners are kept

PREDICT

What do you think will happen to Charity?

throat and looked at the prosecutor. "Now, Mr. Bainbridge, do you have any more questions for this witness?"

"No, Your Honor," Bainbridge replied with a bow.

"Then the witness is excused," the judge ordered.

The prosecution's third and final witness was Abigail Stamford, Charity's younger sister. The shy, blond-haired eleven-year-old was clearly reluctant to testify against her sister, but Judge Gravestone reminded the girl that it was her duty to expose evil wherever she found it, even when it resided under her own roof.

"Earlier this year, you and your sister talked about the future, did you not?" Mr. Bainbridge began gently.

"Yes, sir," young Abigail replied forthrightly, her posture straight, her eyes clear.

◆————————————————————————————◆

"ONE MORE OUTBURST LIKE THAT, AND
I SHALL SEE YOU ALL IN THE STOCKADE!"

◆————————————————————————————◆

"You were talking about what you could be when you grow up, isn't that right?" Mr. Bainbridge probed.

"Yes, sir," Abigail responded.

"And tell me, dear, what did Charity, your older sister, tell you that you could be?" the prosecutor asked, looking disdainfully toward the accused.

"She said I could be anything I wanted," Abigail said painfully.

The spectators responded to this with a collective gasp. Of all the outrageous statements they had heard so far, this was by far the most shocking.

"*She said you could be anything you wanted,*" Mr. Bainbridge repeated, as if unable to believe the statement himself. "Did she mean you could perhaps marry above your station? Or that you could work as a school teacher?"

"No, sir," Abigail replied, a frightened quiver in her voice. "She said that girls should be as equals to boys. That we could grow up to be farmers, physicians, even lawyers and magistrates as we so choose."

At this, Judge Gravestone turned deep red. He looked as if he was about to pop every blood vessel in his stout, flabby body. "Enough!" he finally bellowed. "This court has heard enough!" He turned to Charity. "Miss Stamford, before this court issues its verdict and pronounces its sentence, it shall give you one chance and one chance only to renounce all the blasphemous things you have said."

◆————————————————————◆

"Enough! This court has heard enough!"

◆————————————————————◆

"Sir?" Charity responded, for she did not quite understand the judge's statement.

"I'm giving you a chance to take it all back," Judge Gravestone said imploringly. "All this nonsense about rebellion against the Crown, winged ships, uncensored books, and women magistrates. Deny it all! Tell this court it was nothing but a bad dream! For I can tell you right now, Charity Stamford, that if you don't renounce this heresy this very moment, I will have no choice but to sentence you to death!"

PREDICT

How do you think Charity will respond? What would your response be?

Charity scanned the faces in the room. She saw the fear and contempt in the eyes of the townspeople she thought she knew so well. The agony of her mother. The shame and confusion of her sister Abigail. As a girl who had always devoted her life to truth and honor, she knew what she had to do.

"Very well, Your Honor," she said, sitting tall and looking Judge Gravestone straight in the eye. "I do renounce these claims. They were childish fantasies. Nothing but fairy stories. They have no more weight than the air we breathe."

With that, Judge Gravestone breathed a huge sigh of relief, as did Charity's mother, her sister Abigail, and William Hooke.

"Then all charges are dismissed," the judge declared with a bang of his gavel. "And this court stands <u>adjourned</u>."

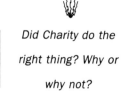

Did Charity do the right thing? Why or why not?

As everyone filed out of the room, Charity's mother and sister ran to the defendant's box and threw their arms around the young girl.

"You foolish child!" her mother said harshly. "How could you talk of such things? You must never, ever speak of the future this way again! You could have gotten us all killed!"

"I am truly sorry, Mother," Charity apologized. "I had no idea these people would react so."

"An entire year in the New World, and you've learned nothing!" her mother chastised her. "Sometimes I wonder why I even bothered to pay for this expedition."

"You said it was for our education," young Abigail reminded her. "To make us understand and appreciate early American history by living a part of it."

adjourned: stopped a meeting for a time

"And instead, you brought glimpses of the future to people who are wholly unable to appreciate it," Charity's mother said. "I fear that if we stay here any longer, we will critically damage the timeline—or worse!"

"I am truly sorry, Mother," Charity said again, bowing her head.

"Tell it to your father when you get home," her mother snapped, then grabbed both her daughters by the arm and hurried them from the building.

◆————————————————————◆

"I AM TRULY SORRY, MOTHER."

◆————————————————————◆

Later that evening, in a cave unknown to the local settlers, Charity, Abigail, and their mother returned to the twenty-first-century time machine that had deposited them here in New England in 1655, one year ago. A few minutes later, they and their vehicle vanished in a brilliant flash of light, never to return.

Unknown to any of them, William Hooke had followed them to this site, and gasped in awe as the Stamfords and their unworldly machine disappeared into thin air. Remembering what Charity *had* said about horseless carriages, free speech, and careers for women, he reached the only logical conclusion he could: Charity had been dealing in the supernatural after all . . . with the aim of confusing and confounding the good people of Massachusetts Bay with visions of a future that could never come to pass.

HERESY

▼ Learning from the Story

What makes stories like "Heresy" so interesting and exciting are their unexpected endings—their plot twists. Working with several other students, see if you can come up with three different endings for "Heresy." Are your plot endings even more twisted than Allen B. Ury's?

▼ Putting It into Practice

You have an idea for your story—a crazy, irrational fear. Now it's time to turn that idea into an outline—a plot. Before you put anything on paper, think your story through in your mind. Then get yourself a stack of note cards. On the first card, write down any ideas you

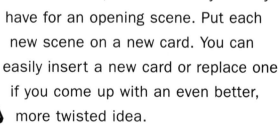

have for an opening scene. Put each new scene on a new card. You can easily insert a new card or replace one if you come up with an even better, more twisted idea.

Post-mortem

It's not uncommon to fear death.
But some people fear life even more.

The last year had been filled with nothing but heartache for fourteen-year-old Stacy Linden and her mother. First, there was the divorce. It had left Stacy, her mother, and her Grandma Doris to get by as best they could, living together in a small rented house on <u>meager</u> welfare and Social Security benefits.

The worst blow had been the sudden death of her grandmother. Stacy had adored the kindly old lady. For Stacy's mother, the shock of suddenly finding herself without both her husband and her mother had been more than she could bear. Often she stayed in bed all day or shuffled listlessly about the house in her robe.

In June, things took a turn for the better. Stacy got a summer job at the law firm of Hartridge and Meyer. She did little more than run errands and file papers, but it was a new beginning and a place away from all the

postmortem: taking place after death

meager: skimpy; very small

unhappiness at home. Stacy liked the people she worked with. She liked the feeling of being on her own, of being independent, and of earning some money. And since she and her mother needed the money so badly, it made her feel good about herself that she could help out.

For a time, even her mother started to perk up, to come to terms with her grief. She took an interest in fixing up their little house, and she even got a part-time job, doing piecework at home as a seamstress.

For the first time in a very, very long time, Stacy began to feel happy. Things were looking up, and Stacy was certain they would only get better. Finally, the future seemed filled with hope and promise.

And then came a phone call at work.

"Stacy, there's a call for you on line one," Mr. Bradshaw, an associate lawyer, told her. "It's your mother. She sounds upset."

A bit worried, Stacy picked up the phone. The voice on the other end of the line sounded like a woman gone mad. Her words made no sense. Her mother cried, then babbled something about a letter—"from your Grandma Doris." At first Stacy was not sure what her mother was talking about. Had her mom come across an old letter from Grandma—one that brought back painful memories?

"No, it's not an *old* letter!" her mother sobbed hysterically. "You don't understand! You don't understand at all!"

Stacy tried to question her further, but her mother began sobbing and was unable to continue. There was a loud click as she hung up.

Not until she got home that evening, anxious and troubled, did Stacy begin to understand.

"I found this on my desk!" cried her mother, waving a piece of pink stationery in Stacy's face. Stacy took the paper and read out loud: "*I'm so lonely, my darling, so lost without you. Come to me.*" The message was written in what looked like her grandmother's flowery handwriting . . . but it *couldn't* be.

"There's no date," Stacy pointed out. "When do you think it was written?"

Her mother sat down. Her face was a tight, twisted mask. She began rocking back and forth.

"Mom," Stacy coaxed. "Try to think. Do you have any idea when this could have been written?"

The answer was a wailing shriek. "Today!" her mother screeched, continuing to rock, tugging and twisting at a lock of her hair.

"That's not possible, Mother," said Stacy as evenly as she could. "I'm sure it's some sort of—" She struggled to find the right word. "Just some sort of *mistake*."

Her mother shook her head violently. "There's no mistake about it. This letter was written today."

Stacy put a hand on her mother's shoulder. "Grandma didn't write that letter, at least not today. She's dead, Mom. Grandma is dead."

Who do you think really wrote that letter?

Her mother stared into space. "Yes," she said, her voice a hollow monotone. "But the dead never leave us."

"Mother—!"

"Don't you see?" her mother interrupted, taking Stacy's hand. "She's trying to communicate with me, to reach me. She needs me, Stacy. My mother needs me!"

"But Grandma's dead!" Stacy blurted, fighting the fear rising within her.

Her mother smiled strangely. "But she's calling out to me."

Stacy put her arms around her mother. "You're lonely, Mom. I understand because I'm lonely, too. This has been hard on both of us. But we can't let it get to us, or make us imagine things." She forced a smile. "Mom, dead people don't write letters."

Her mother just looked at her with an odd, faraway look in her eyes.

✳ ✳ ✳

But with each passing day, things became worse. More ugly. More insane.

Almost unbearable.

There were more letters from her grandmother. And more phone calls to Stacy at work from her mother. The calls shattered her nerves, often leaving her in tears.

The calls and the change in Stacy's behavior did not go unnoticed by her fellow workers.

One day, after her mother had called three times, the floor manager, Ms. Trump, took Stacy aside. "I don't mean to pry into your personal life," she said, "nor do I really understand what's going on. But these phone calls from your mother are interfering with your work."

Stacy apologized and promised the calls would stop.

Which they did—when Stacy demanded that her mother leave her alone at work. That's when things at home got worse.

Now, every day when Stacy came home she was greeted by a crazy woman. A woman who sometimes ranted and raved. Or sat hunched over, reading and rereading letters on pink stationery. Letters supposedly from her Grandma Doris, who was dead and buried but somehow still with them, now as a dark and <u>sinister</u> part of their lives.

With each day, Stacy's heart broke again when she walked into the house and saw her mother. The poor woman ate almost nothing. Her bones showed. Her back was bent over more and more each day. Her face had become pale and waxy looking. Her eyes, sunken and vacant looking, were forever moving restlessly, as if looking for someone—for Grandma Doris—to appear.

Always complaining of one ailment or another, her mother had quit her work as a seamstress, too, and returned to her old ways. Once again she stayed in bed most of the day or wandered about in her shabby robe, her pockets stuffed with dozens of letters on pink stationery.

Stacy begged her to go see a doctor, to get help. But the pleas had only brought on fits of yelling and tears, followed by long hours of <u>torturous</u>, icy silence.

Only at work did Stacy find any peace. Only there did she have any purpose, any freedom from the ugliness of her home life. She felt guilty, but she no longer wanted to go home. As often as she could, she volunteered to work overtime.

Late one afternoon, the last bit of normalcy left Stacy's life. She would never forget how the whole office plunged into silence when the doors burst open and her mother, clad in her robe and slippers, stormed in. Her hair hung in dirty ringlets. Her fevered, glassy eyes searched out—then riveted on—Stacy. As her mother

sinister: evil

torturous: strained and painful

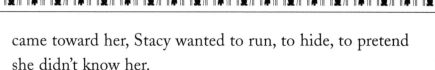

came toward her, Stacy wanted to run, to hide, to pretend she didn't know her.

Why is Stacy's mother acting this way?

Stacy's face was red with embarrassment, and there were tears in her eyes. Her mother stood before her, pulled a pink paper from her robe, and read: "*Your mother needs you. Come to me. Come to me now!*"

Two secretaries said something in an undertone. Someone coughed. Then, seemingly startled, as though realizing for the first time where she was, Stacy's mother gathered her robe about herself as she stared, wide-eyed, at the stunned office workers. Then she turned and walked back through the silent office and out the door.

Stacy ran to the ladies' room to cry . . . and to hide.

Stacy did not wait to be fired. She quit that afternoon. The embarrassment of it all was just too great. She could never show her face there again.

Instead of taking the bus home that horrible day, Stacy walked all the way home. It was a good five miles, and the evening was hot and very humid. She was exhausted and sticky with perspiration when she finally got home.

All was dark and strangely still in the house. "Mother!" she called out. There was no reply. Stacy made her way from room to room, flipping on lights as she went.

She found her mother sitting at her desk in her bedroom, her back to the door.

"Why, Mother?" Stacy asked. "Why did you do that to me?"

Her mother remained motionless.

Stacy was filled with sorrow and compassion. Her anger drained from her. She walked over and put a hand on her mother's shoulder. The swivel chair turned and her mother slumped to one side, her glazed eyes fixed on some distant point. She was dead. "Mother!" Stacy screamed, again and again and again.

※　※　※

On the way back from the funeral, the lady from the child welfare department talked about Stacy's future and about the McLeish Home for Girls, where Stacy would be staying until foster parents could be found for her. Or, Mrs. Canfield had wondered aloud, "Perhaps some arrangement can be worked out with your father?"

Stacy shook her head. "No, I'm better off without him. He doesn't care about me any more than he cared about my mother. He wasn't even at the funeral!"

Mrs. Canfield looked uncomfortable. "I don't know all the details, but I can see you've been through a lot." She smiled at Stacy warmly. "Things will start looking up— you'll see."

Stacy brushed back a tear. "I'll be okay," she said in a slightly quavering voice.

At the house, Mrs. Canfield helped Stacy tote two suitcases and several boxes of belongings out to the car. On the way to the McLeish Home for Girls, Mrs. Canfield stopped and treated Stacy to lunch. Afterward, they went for a walk together in the park. Stacy liked Mrs. Canfield. She told her all about what had happened—about her grandmother, her mother, and about the letters and her mother's going mad. "My mom's at peace now," she said.

※　※　※

The following week, Mrs. Canfield and Stacy returned to the house. New renters would be moving in, and something would have to be done with her mother's

PREDICT

Will Stacy's life improve now? What will happen to her?

clothing and other belongings. Except for a few keepsakes, Stacy decided everything should go to charity. Together, she and Mrs. Canfield stacked boxes on the front porch.

It was dark and dusky by the time they finished, and Mrs. Canfield sat down on the porch stairs to rest.

Stacy went back into the house to take one last look around. All was so quiet, so deathly quiet. Especially her mother's bedroom. The place sent chills down her spine. But a few last things had to be done . . . including cleaning out that desk.

Stacy left the pencils, pens, erasers, and paper clips where she had found them in the top drawer. In another drawer she found magazines, newspaper clippings, and a few old photographs. She put the photographs in her purse, and the rest went into the wastebasket.

But it was the bottom drawer that took all of Stacy's willpower to clean. From it she pulled a half-empty box of stationery and a stack of papers. Most were letters, the letters that had driven her mother mad.

Tears fell from Stacy's eyes as, one by one, she tore up the letters and threw them into the wastebasket.

The blank stationery frightened and upset her as much as the letters. She hated it, wanted to be rid of it, to be done, once and for all, with every last reminder of the insanity that had destroyed her mother. She grabbed the box, and suddenly she was overcome with grief. Her hands shook violently. "Mother!" she cried. "No!" The box fell from her hands, and pink stationery scattered across the desktop.

A voice came from far away, from outside. "Stacy, we'd better get a move on," Mrs. Canfield called from somewhere out front.

For a moment Stacy's head cocked in the direction of Mrs. Canfield's voice. Then she glanced back at the desk.

"Stacy?" called the faint voice.

But Stacy said nothing. She gripped the armrest of the chair, her eyes fixed on a pink sheet of stationery.

The handwriting was tight, and cramped looking. It was her mother's writing. Slowly, words formed across the background of pink. "No," Stacy whispered. "Mother, please, no."

Mrs. Canfield rushed into the room. "What's wrong?" she asked. "Are you all right?"

Stacy's gaze traveled slowly from the piece of stationery to Mrs. Canfield. Slowly, Stacy handed the woman the piece of pink paper.

Mrs. Canfield read out loud: "*Now you understand, my darling daughter. I miss you so much, love you so much. Come to me, my love, please come.*"

"Stacy, did you write this?" asked Mrs. Canfield. "Stacy? Stacy!" Mrs. Canfield began to shake her. "Stacy, who wrote this?"

But Stacy said nothing. She looked up at the woman. Her face slowly twisted into an odd smile. Her eyes were glassy, filled with horror. And the dawning of madness.

Dead Man's Handle

A voice from the dead is nothing to fear—is it?

"**B**reaker, <u>breaker</u>, this is Boy Wonder. Anyone out there?"

Glen was sitting in the driver's seat of the old black car parked in the steeply sloped driveway behind his house. It was his dad's car, the one he drove when he wasn't working . . . before the accident.

Glen's dad had been a trucker. He used to drive a big <u>rig</u> around the country until that horrible night, months ago, when his mom had gotten the call telling her he'd been in an accident. Glen distinctly remembered the way his mom had slumped against the wall, and he had known instantly that his dad wouldn't be coming back home ever again.

He and his mom lived alone, way out in the country, far from any other house, making it hard for Glen to see his friends very often. Before the accident, that didn't matter. When Glen got lonely, he'd sit in his dad's car, get on the CB radio, and try to contact him on the road. Now when Glen was lonely, he sat in the car looking for *anyone* to talk to. He used the handle, or nickname, his dad had given him years ago—Boy Wonder.

"Breaker, breaker. Boy Wonder here," Glen said into the mouthpiece. "Anyone out there? Over."

breaker, breaker: a CB radio term used to start a conversation

rig: a tractor and trailer used to haul cargo across the country

Suddenly a voice crackled back at him through the speaker. "I read you, Boy Wonder. Loud and clear. Over." The voice was familiar.

"Who am I talking to?" Glen asked.

"Who are you talking to?" The astonishment in the voice was obvious. "This is Red Dog, you lunkhead."

Glen sat up straight in the seat. *Red Dog?* The hair rose on the back of his neck. That was his *dad's* handle.

"Are you there, Boy Wonder?"

"Is—is that you, Dad?"

"Sure is. I'm coming to—" The voice broke up in a crackle of static.

"But Dad, you're—" Glen couldn't bring himself to say the word.

"Late? I know, son. Couldn't be helped. But I'm on my way now. I'm on Pine Ridge Road."

Pine Ridge? Glen thought quickly. *That's less than a mile away.*

Glen's mom wouldn't talk to him about his dad's death, but Glen found out it had been a horrible accident when he read a letter his mom had written to her sister. Apparently his dad was so mangled that his mom could identify the body only from the shirt he was wearing.

"I'll be there soon, son. You still reading me?"

Glen looked down the road and saw headlights coming. "But Dad, I—I don't—"

"No buts, boy. Sit tight and don't move. Everything's going to be okay."

How does this dialogue help you understand these two characters?

The headlights were getting closer. They were definitely the headlights from a big rig. Glen watched, his heart pounding.

Suddenly the brakes of the old car gave out. In a split second, the car rolled down the steep driveway and out onto the country road, where it came to a stop. Glen scrambled for the driver's side door and pushed, but it didn't budge— no one had driven the car for so long the door was jammed.

Now the enormous headlights were almost upon Glen. But then, from the *opposite* direction, he heard the shrill blast of an air horn. He turned just in time to see *another* set of headlights closing in on him! *I'm about to be crushed between two trucks!* Glen's mind screamed.

He turned back and saw the first set of headlights swerve out of the way to avoid the other oncoming truck. Then the huge red big rig whooshed by, missing the car Glen was in by inches.

Glen spun around and saw the *second* set of headlights almost upon him. He raised his eyes to the cab and saw a familiar face—it was his dad! Then, just before it reached him, the truck suddenly vanished.

"That was a close call, good buddy," his dad's voice crackled over the CB. "Next time you're on your own. Don't forget to push that old car off the road. Over and out."

"Dad!" Glen cried into the radio. "Dad!"

But the radio in his hand was dead, and Glen was overcome with grief, for he knew that his dad had come back for one last job, and now it was over.

PREDICT

What will happen to Glen? What details from the story make you think as you do?

Postmortem

▼ **Learning from the Story**

Good characters are like the kid next door—you feel as if you've known them all your life. Choose a character from either "Postmortem" or "Dead Man's Handle." On one half of a sheet of paper, write down all the things you know about that character from the story. On the other half, write down two or three other things you think you know about that character, based on your experience with similar people.

▼ **Putting It into Practice**

A police artist can piece together a very realistic picture of a criminal based on just a few telling characteristics. Work with someone who can draw well. Tell that person all about the main character in your own nightmarish story. As you talk, make a list of everything you tell the artist as she or he tries to draw a picture of your character. Keep adding details until the drawing looks like the character you had in mind. Be sure to keep the drawing and your notes in your story file.

Monkeys TONIGHT.

My sister wakes up screaming at the top of her lungs—a sharp, shrill sound, like an alarm, or a teakettle boiling to death. The awful noise rips me out of the deepest of sleeps. I twist through space until I feel the blanket around me and the coldness of my feet. She screams again, and I pull the blanket over my head, trying to cram it into my ears.

Then I hear the panicked footsteps of my parents as they race down the hall. I glance at the clock. It's almost four in the morning.

Mom and Dad bound into the room as Melinda empties her lungs again, even louder than before.

"Shut her up!" I croak to my parents in a <u>raspy</u> night voice. Mom and Dad ignore me and race to Melinda's bed. They shake her and shake her until she comes out of her nightmare. Her screaming fades to a whimper, but when she sees Mom and Dad above her, she begins to sob. Dad takes her into his arms as she cries.

"I'll get her some water," says Mom.

"Bring some for me," I say, knowing that Mom doesn't hear me. She never hears me when Smellinda is crying.

What causes nightmares? Pepperoni pizza? A spicy burrito? Or maybe your own imagination?

raspy: harsh; scratchy

Smellinda: that's what I call her because, as far as I'm concerned, she stinks.

"Can't you shut her up?" I plead, trying to stretch the blanket over my freezing feet.

"Michelle, just go back to sleep," says Dad.

Easy for him to say. He doesn't have to share a room with a human air-raid siren. There is something wrong when a twelve-year-old girl is forced to share a room with her eight-year-old sister. There ought to be a law against it.

Dad picks up Melinda and rocks her gently. "What is it, honey?" he asks.

"Monkeys," whimpers Melinda.

I groan and bury my head in my pillow as Mom brings water for Melinda and nothing for me. Why did I know it was going to be monkeys? It's always monkeys.

Monkeys. Of all the dumb things to be afraid of. I mean, there are plenty of *really* scary things to be afraid of, aren't there? Mummies, and skeletons, and spooky graveyards, and vampires. Personally, it's spiders that freak me out. Sometimes I imagine these big, three-foot-long spiders with hairy black legs the size of human arms. They drink your blood, spiders do. Well, not human blood—fly blood. But I suppose if spiders were big enough, they could go for human blood, too. Just the thought of them makes my skin crawl and my heart start to race. But *monkeys?* Who in their right mind is scared of monkeys?

How does Michelle feel about Melinda?

Smellinda, that's who.

Dad holds her and walks back and forth on Melinda's side of the room, full of dolls and rainbow wallpaper. It's

the side of the room my friends make fun of when they come over to visit, as if I had anything to say about it.

"There are no monkeys in here," Dad tells Melinda. "It was just a dream. Just your imagination."

"They came down the chimney," she cries. I start to laugh to myself. A few weeks ago we saw a television show about how they transport zoo animals by plane. One of the animals they showed was a monkey. Ever since then, Melinda is certain that every time a plane flies by, a monkey is going to jump out of the plane like a hairy <u>paratrooper</u> and head straight for our chimney.

"There are no monkeys in the room, sweet cakes," says Mom, flicking on the light, blinding me. "See?"

I roll over and bury my face in the pillow.

"The closet," says my sister.

Dad opens the closet to reveal clothes and a messy pile of toys.

"The bathroom," says Melinda.

Dad steps into the bathroom, peeling back the shower curtain to reveal just a leaky faucet and a bathtub ring.

"The kitchen," insists Melinda.

Dad carries her down the hallway, and I hear him and Mom inspect every inch of our house. Closets, cabinets, the oven, the fireplace—they even check under the furniture.

Finally, ten minutes later, they come back with Melinda happily asleep in Dad's arms, satisfied that the house has been <u>purged</u> of the banana-eating menaces. They gently tuck her in, turn off the light, and go back to bed.

Melinda, her nose stuffy from crying, snores away. Even after her monkey fit, she can sleep. But I'm not so

paratrooper: a soldier who uses a parachute to jump from a plane

purged: cleared out; gotten rid of

lucky. I can hear everything around me. I hear the awful ticking of her Mickey Mouse clock. I hear the *whap!* as the paper boy throws newspapers on driveways long before the sun comes up. When I open my eyes, I see shadows and get spooked. The shadows are like fat spiders, with legs stretching along the walls and floor. Darkness creeping, inch by inch, toward my bed. I know that it's only clothes piled in the corner and stuffed animals on the shelves and patterns cast by the window blind, but still, I see spiders. Once I've got the spider creeps, I know I won't sleep for the rest of the night, no matter how much I want to.

But there's Melinda across the room, sleeping happily with her dolls and purple ponies and fluffy teddy bears. She sleeps peacefully, probably dreaming of a beautiful fairy-tale castle. And I silently wish for her dream castle to be invaded by baboons.

How would this story change if Melinda were the narrator?

On the drive to school in the morning, Melinda and I sit in the backseat. Melinda plays with her Deep Space Betty doll, who has blue hair and green skin. I just sit there like a zombie who didn't get enough sleep. How I wish I could go back to bed!

Mom drives, listening to the news, hoping to hear a traffic report. Instead, we hear a story about the zoo.

Tragedy struck at the Central Zoo yesterday, begins the reporter, *when an angry gorilla apparently broke through its cage, grabbed a man, and ripped off—*

CLICK!

Mom quickly turns off the radio, pretending she didn't hear the reporter.

Melinda looks at me with a face that's turning almost as green as Deep Space Betty. "Ripped off what?" she asks.

"Probably ripped off his arms," I tell her.

"Michelle!" my mother warns.

"Maybe his head, too. Gorillas are known to do that."

"Mommy, what do you think the gorilla ripped off?" Melinda asks <u>tentatively</u>.

"I think it ripped off his wallet," says Mom, "so it could treat *Mrs.* Gorilla to a fancy dinner."

Melinda laughs.

"Maybe got his legs, too," I tell Melinda. "Apes are strong. Monkeys are, too. I'll bet if they wanted to, all the gorillas and baboons and orangutans and chimps could break out of their cages and escape in a matter of minutes. Hey, Mom, how far is the zoo from our house?"

"Never mind that!" says Mom.

I snicker, and in a flash of inspiration, I grab Melinda's Deep Space Betty. "This is probably how it looked at the zoo yesterday." I insert Betty hair-first into my mouth and bite off her head.

"*Mommmmyyyyyyy!*" screams Melinda.

Mom glares at me in the rear-view mirror. "Michelle, stop it!" she yells.

I spit out the little plastic head and it <u>ricochets</u> off the window and lands in Melinda's lap. She puts the head back on, but she can't stop crying. I, on the other hand, can't stop laughing.

tentatively: uncertainly; hesitantly

ricochets: bounces back

It's a full moon tonight. The kind that brings out the werewolves—if you believe in that stuff. Our house doesn't get werewolves, though. Tonight, we get something else.

I'm fast asleep when I first hear Melinda. She's not screaming; she's calling my name. "Michelle," she whispers. I'm dragged feet first out of my dream and twist through space back into my bed, where I open my eyes and see Melinda looking toward me in the dim blue of the moonlit room. It is four o'clock again. I sigh and wish there were a Sister Fairy who would come in the night to take Melinda away, leaving a quarter beneath my pillow. Fair exchange.

"Michelle," she whispers. "Do you hear that?"

Scrape, scrape, scrape. It could be coming from anywhere.

"It's probably just a stray cat," I tell her. "Go to sleep." But the sound gets louder. *Scrape! Scrape! Scrape!* Now I can hear the hiss and rattle of falling <u>debris</u>.

"It's coming from the chimney!" says Melinda.

"Naah, it's probably just Dad making some weird late-night snack," I say, but now the sound has got me worried, too.

I sit up and listen. There's a noise coming from the hardwood floor in the living room. The squishy sound of bare feet—*plod-plod-plod*—but then the sound is gone. *It's in the hallway,* I tell myself. *It's walking on the carpeted hallway, silently.*

It's much too quiet. I can hear the ticking of the clock pounding in my ears like a woodpecker. I am about to announce to Melinda that it was just her imagination when a shadow leaps into the room, howling.

debris: the remains of something broken or destroyed

What do you think it is?

It's a monkey—laughing in a crazy, screeching, evil voice. I see it, but I don't believe it. I am too shocked to scream.

"Michelle?" Melinda's high-pitched, panicked voice is like a squeaky wheel. "No . . . no," she whines. She tries to scream, but it's like her throat is all closed up in fear. She starts batting the air around her. "Go away! Go away!"

A second monkey runs into the room, jumps up on a shelf, and begins throwing books everywhere.

Another monkey comes in through the window and terrorizes Melinda, <u>flailing</u> its hands in her face and making awful noises. Melinda gasps, unable to catch her breath in fear. Then she screams, and so do I. That's when the room explodes into a mad monkeyhouse. The closet door flies open and they leap out like <u>commandos</u>—not just monkeys, but apes like chimpanzees and orangutans, too. They charge out of the closet as if the closet is a doorway to another world. Small monkeys with long tails and white faces climb out of the dresser drawers and leap from wall to wall. A single gorilla growls in the doorway, making sure we can't get out. Both of us scream and scream. *Where are our parents? Why can't we hear them coming down the hall?*

One baboon with wild, fiery eyes and sharpened teeth smiles and speaks—*he actually speaks!* "Your parents won't wake up," he sneers. "They won't wake up until morning. We won't let them."

I try to help Melinda, but hairy hands grab me and throw me back against the wall. I can only watch as they torment her, tearing apart her stuffed animals, chewing them to bits, shredding her books, leaping across her bed,

flailing: waving about wildly

commandos: soldiers who make daring raids on enemy territory

and swinging wildly through the room. They pull at her arms and tug at her hair as she screams. An orangutan plays her head like the bongo drums. A chimp makes hideous faces at her, and Melinda keeps screaming in terror, until she finally screams herself out. Soon her voice is gone, but her mouth keeps screaming silently. This is her nightmare—but how did it get out of her head? *How?*

Finally the raid ends, and the apes and monkeys begin to leave. Some climb out of the window, others vanish into the closet, some climb into the dresser drawers and disappear, and others race out of the room and scurry up the chimney. I look at Melinda. She is pale. She looks straight ahead, frozen, but does not see.

"Melinda?

She will not answer me. It's as if she's gone far away and doesn't even hear me.

"Melinda?"

But she won't talk at all. I think she may never talk again.

The last monkey—the baboon with sharpened teeth— looks around at the ruined room, at the night's work. He leaps up to the windowsill to leave, and I say a prayer of thanks that it's all over. But then he turns to me before he disappears into the night. He smiles at me, showing his terrible teeth. I pull my blanket over me, but it won't cover my feet no matter how hard I try.

"Pleasant dreams, Michelle," he rasps in a deep, scratchy voice. Then he says, with an awful wink:

"Tomorrow night, spiders."

How do you think Michelle will feel about her sister now?

Monkeys TONIGHT

▼ Learning from the Story

"Monkeys Tonight" is told from twelve-year-old Michelle's point of view. How different would the story be if someone not in the story, an outside narrator, told it? Working with several other students, retell the story. Take turns describing the events through the eyes of a third-person narrator. How does the story change? You might want to tell the story again—this time from Melinda's point of view.

▼ Putting It into Practice

Try telling a partner about a scene from your nightmarish story. Describe the scene as if it happened to you. Keep in mind that you can only talk about things that you saw and did. Does the story work that way? If so, you might consider telling your story from a first-person point of view.

If you have trouble explaining the events, you might want to tell your story from a third-person point of view.

The Stray

You never know who—or what—is going to follow you home from school!

Louisa McBride had been warned repeatedly not to take the shortcut home from school. Although walking around the long-abandoned Jerry's Jumbo Mart on Lafayette Avenue could shave an entire block off her trip, the route was considered far too dangerous for a thirteen-year-old girl to travel alone.

"It's not safe," her mother told her on more than one occasion. "It's dirty and probably rat infested. Who knows what diseases you could pick up there?"

"And there are lots of dark places for people to hide," her father always noted. "Don't even think about walking around that old store."

And Louisa usually *didn't* think about it, even when she stayed late at school and was eager to get home, even when the day was so bright and sunny that dangers, if any, would be easily visible from hundreds of feet away. No, usually Louisa obeyed her parents and walked all the way around the block, even going so far as to travel on the opposite sidewalk. The truth was, the old boarded-up building gave her the creeps, and she wanted to stay as far away from it as she could.

Her friend, Judy MacDougal, however, was not so
skittish. In fact, Judy was known throughout their junior
high as something of a daredevil. Years before, she had been
the first girl in their circle of friends to try the high dive at
the downtown community center pool. More recently, she'd
been the first in line to ride the new quadruple-loop
"Devastator" roller coaster at the nearby Sea Cliffs theme
park. And to everyone's amazement, for her thirteenth
birthday, she actually went skydiving with her father.

In light of Judy's reputation for fearlessness, it came as
no surprise to Louisa when one fateful Thursday afternoon
Judy suggested they take the shortcut past the old
abandoned supermarket. They'd been assigned to work
together on a school history project and were going to
Louisa's house to study when a storm moved in.

"Let's cut through the lot," Judy suggested, pointing to
the empty parking area alongside Jerry's Jumbo Mart.
"Hurry, it's going to pour!"

"But I'm not allowed to walk through there," Louisa
reminded her friend. "It's too dangerous."

"Climbing out of bed in the morning is dangerous,"
Judy countered, already starting to cross the street.
"Besides, I really don't think there are any mad killers
lurking in the shadows, getting cold and wet."

"But if my folks find out, they'll kill me!" Louisa
explained, joining Judy on the opposite side of the street
against her will.

"So who's going to tell them?" Judy asked. Not waiting
for an answer, she headed into the lot. "I mean, come on,
Louisa, eventually a girl has to start thinking for herself."

skittish: easily
frightened

*Should Louisa take
the shortcut? Why or
why not?*

Louisa hesitated only a moment before running after her friend. Part of her felt positively terrified as she imagined all kinds of horrors hiding behind the broken windows and the overflowing dumpsters, waiting to jump out and grab her as she hurried past. But another part of her felt strangely <u>exhilarated</u> as she courageously faced danger head-on.

Racing to catch up to Judy, who was now walking confidently down the service alley that ran along the west side of the store, Louisa shuddered. This was the spookiest part of the trip, as the pathway narrowed quickly to form a long, dark alley with the abandoned supermarket on one side and a high brick wall on the other. The alley was filled with piles of long-forgotten grocery store refuse left there by other kids who'd come this way previously. If a person was going to be attacked, this is where it would happen.

"Come on, what are you waiting for?" Judy cried as she motioned for Louisa to hurry up. <u>Steeling</u> herself, Louisa was just pulling up to Judy's side when a dark form jumped into the path in front of them. Louisa's heart nearly stopped as she saw what appeared to be a huge wolf standing not ten feet away, its yellowish eyes glowing in the dim, shadowy twilight.

Louisa stopped short and clutched Judy's arm. "What are we going to do?" she squeaked in <u>mortal</u> terror.

"Oh, calm down," Judy said, shaking free of Louisa's grasp. "It's just a dumb old dog."

Indeed, as Louisa turned her attention back to the beast, she saw that the "wolf" was in fact just a large brown mutt. About the size of a small German shepherd,

exhilarated: excited

steeling: strengthening; preparing for conflict or danger

mortal: extreme; deadly

he had no collar or other means of identification. His short-haired coat was dirty from months of neglect, and he had a large scar over his right eye, most likely the result of some territorial dog fight. His eyes, though, were bright and warm, and he seemed genuinely happy to see these two human visitors.

"Let's get out of here," Louisa said softly, pulling Judy back the way they'd come. "Don't let him touch you. He's probably covered with germs. He might even have rabies!"

"Oh, stop being such a wuss!" Judy scoffed. Slowly, she walked forward, her right hand extended palm upward. "Hey, doggy," she said in a soft, babylike voice. "You look like a good dog. Are you happy to see me?"

Louisa was amazed at Judy's courage. Louisa never approached strange dogs, even those who belonged to her own friends. After all, you never knew when one would take a move or gesture the wrong way and go straight for your throat. Yet, here was Judy, not only standing her ground against an unknown stray, but actually trying to make friends with him. It was an act of courage—or stupidity—that would only add to the girl's already legendary reputation.

As Louisa watched in awe, the dog inched cautiously forward, sniffed Judy's hand, then gave it a gentle lick. Judy stroked the dog's head, and he sat down to enjoy the attention.

"It looks like you've made a friend," Louisa said, giving a nervous laugh.

"Animals like me," Judy replied, now scratching the dog behind his ears. "They can tell I'm harmless." Then she motioned Louisa to join her. "You try it. I promise, he won't bite."

Still anxious, Louisa carefully approached the dog and half-heartedly held out her right hand. But as soon as the dog turned his attention to her, Louisa fearfully pulled her hand away.

"Oh, stop it, you big baby!" Judy scolded. "I told you, the dog will not bite you. He's as gentle as a pussycat!"

Once again, Louisa reached her hand toward the dog. This time, the animal actually lowered his head to allow her to stroke him. Louisa laid her palm on top of the dog's large head, then gently petted the back of his neck. The fur was warm, soft, and inviting. In fact, it felt so good, Louisa petted the dog a second, then a third time.

"Ooo, you *are* a good dog," she cooed. At this the dog perked up and licked Louisa's fingertips. Louisa could have stayed there all day, but at that moment a cold wind whipped through the alley and the rain started to fall <u>in earnest</u>. "We'd better get out of here," she said to Judy urgently. "See you later, boy," she added to the dog, then the two girls moved quickly through the remainder of the alley.

They were almost to Michigan Street, which would take them straight to Louisa's house, when they noticed that the dog was following them. Judy waved her hand at the animal, trying to shoo it away. "Go home!" she ordered. "You can't come with us. Go on. Get out of here!" But the dog refused to retreat, following them at a distance of fifteen to twenty feet all the way home.

The rain was falling steadily when the girls finally arrived at Louisa's house. Opening her front door, Louisa

Are you more like Judy or Louisa? How are you like her?

in earnest: seriously; very hard

turned back and saw the dog standing on the sidewalk, looking at her with sad, pleading eyes, like it wanted nothing more than to come inside and get out of the dampness. Louisa sympathized with the animal's plight but knew that her parents would never allow an animal— let alone a stray—into their house.

"Sorry, boy," she said sadly, "but you can't come in. Go home. Go back where you came from."

Just then, Louisa's mother appeared in the <u>foyer</u>. "What are you girls doing?" she asked, seeing the two standing in the open doorway. "Come inside. It's pouring out there." It was then she, too, noticed the dog standing at the edge of their lawn. "What's *that*?" she asked.

"He followed us home," Louisa said quickly, careful to make no mention of the supermarket. "I think it's a stray."

"Well, just ignore it and it'll go away," her mother advised. "Now come inside and dry yourselves off."

Louisa took one last, painful glance back at the dog before entering the house and closing the door. Deep in her heart, she wished that she could at least allow the animal to come inside and wait out the storm. That was, after all, the humane thing to do. But she knew her mother would be dead set against allowing the beast to set even one paw inside their house, so she made no further mention of it, telling herself that the dog had obviously spent most of his life on the streets and was probably used to it.

However, when six o'clock arrived and it was time for Judy to leave, Louisa was surprised to see that the stray was now camped out on their front stoop. He was just lying there peacefully, sheltered from the storm by the

foyer: front hallway

overhanging roof. Louisa's mother, who was preparing to drive Judy home, was equally surprised to find the uninvited guest, and also a little annoyed.

"I'd better call Animal Control," she said, heading for the kitchen telephone.

"Wait!" Louisa insisted. "Can't we keep him? I've always wanted a dog, and I promise to take care of him."

Louisa's mother considered her daughter's request. "I had no idea you wanted a dog," she finally said. "I suppose we can discuss this with your father when he gets home. Then, if you'd like, we can go to a pet store."

"But I want *this* dog," Louisa cried. "He needs me."

Again, Louisa's mother paused before giving her a reply. She looked down at the mutt, who in turn looked back with his two big, sad, watery eyes.

"Well, all right," she said hesitantly. "If your father says it's okay with him, then it's okay with me."

As if understanding that he had just found a home, the dog suddenly jumped up onto his hind legs and began licking Louisa's face.

"Looks like you've got a friend," Judy said with a chuckle. "So what are you going to call him?"

Louisa thought about this for a moment, then replied, "Jerry."

How do you think Jerry feels about being adopted? How can you tell?

Over the next month, Louisa and Jerry became the best of buddies. Although Louisa's parents originally insisted the dog be kept in the back yard, the <u>wily</u> animal used his big, sad puppy-dog eyes to get himself invited into the house and, finally, into Louisa's bedroom, where he took no time making himself comfortable.

Every morning, Louisa got up fifteen minutes earlier than usual so she'd have enough time to feed and walk Jerry before she had to leave for school. When she came home, she fed and walked the dog again, then studied with him resting at her feet. At night, Jerry slept at the foot of Louisa's bed, which gave the girl a sense of warmth and security she'd never felt before.

And then, about a month after Jerry had moved into the McBride home, he and Louisa were walking through nearby Morningstar Park when the dog suddenly bolted away so fast that he yanked his leash clear out of the girl's hand. Before Louisa knew what was happening, Jerry was racing across the grass at full speed as if he was chasing after some invisible prey.

"Jerry! Come back!" Louisa shouted, running after the dog. "Stop!"

At the edge of the park, the dog finally stopped and glanced back, waiting for Louisa to catch up with him. "Bad dog!" Louisa scolded. "Don't you *ever* do that again!"

She was reaching down for Jerry's leash when the unpredictable dog took off again, this time barking wildly as he raced into the street. Becoming more and more distressed, Louisa chased after the animal, terrified that he'd get hit by a car.

wily: sly; crafty

At the next corner, Jerry stopped again and waited for Louisa to catch up. Then, just as before, he took off as soon as she was about to take hold of his leash. It went on like this for block after endless block, the dog apparently making sure he remained free while at the same time making equally certain that Louisa never lost sight of him.

Where is Jerry headed? How do you know?

Finally, the chase led them to Lafayette Avenue. Barking tauntingly, Jerry dashed into the abandoned Jerry's Jumbo Mart parking lot, raced toward the side alley, then disappeared into the building through a broken window.

"Jerry!" Louisa cried breathlessly, tears welling in her eyes. "Jerry, please come back! Come on, boy! Come out of there!"

Afraid that she'd lost her pet forever, Louisa slowly made her way toward the opening through which Jerry had entered the building. Stepping carefully to avoid the broken glass that lay strewn all over the pavement, she peered into the dim grayness of the abandoned store's interior, then called the dog again.

She heard a distant bark, and hope rose in her heart. Barely considering her parents' warnings to stay away from this place, she squeezed herself through the narrow opening and continued on in pursuit of her dog.

In the years that had passed since the store went out of business, an inch-thick layer of dust had settled over everything, and leaks in the roof had caused many sections of the old linoleum floor to crack and rot.

"Jerry?" Louisa called hesitantly as she made her way up one of the aisles past rows and rows of empty shelves. "Where are you, boy?"

Suddenly, something flashed by at the end of the aisle, then disappeared from sight. "Jerry?" Louisa called again, starting after the <u>elusive</u> animal.

But as she did, a section of the floor beneath her groaned and abruptly gave way. Louisa screamed and flailed her arms wildly as she suddenly found herself falling through a huge hole in the floor. Then, a moment later—WHAM!—she landed on a hard surface while bits of debris rained down on her.

Looking around, Louisa saw that she had fallen into some kind of basement storage area. Painfully struggling to her feet, she moved through the inky darkness until she found a door at one end of the room . . . but it was locked tight.

"Help!" she shouted up toward the hole she'd fallen through. "Can anyone hear me? I'm trapped down here in the basement!"

She waited for a reply but heard nothing. Now she was getting *really* scared. Here she was, trapped in a dark, damp basement that was probably filled with rats, spiders, and who-knew-what-else, and there wasn't another human being anywhere around. Even when her parents realized she was missing and started looking for her, they'd never think to look in Jerry's Jumbo Mart. After all, they'd forbidden her countless times to even go near this awful place.

I could die down here of thirst and starvation, Louisa thought frantically. *It could be weeks before anyone even finds my remains!*

Just then, Louisa heard movement behind her, and spinning around in terror, she saw two yellowish eyes

elusive: cleverly avoiding

PREDICT

What do you think will happen to Louisa?

glowing within the gloom. But almost in the same moment, she realized they held no danger.

"Jerry!" she sighed with relief. "How did you get down here? Did you come to save me?"

The next moment, two more glowing eyes appeared next to Jerry's. Then another pair appeared to her left, and another to her right. Her heart pounding in her ears, Louisa realized that she was *surrounded* by wild dogs, all of whom were staring at her like <u>predators</u> preparing for the kill. Only one thought now occupied Louisa's mind: *How many more seconds do I have to live?*

✳ ✳ ✳

What are you doing with this human? the large female dog asked her offspring in a combination of sounds and movements that only dogs understand. *What is it doing in our home?*

predators: animals that attack, destroy, and eat other animals

It followed me home, Mother, the mutt known as "Jerry" replied. *It likes me. Can I keep it?*

The mother considered her offspring's request for a moment, then gave a short, high-pitched whine that meant, *We'll ask your father. If it's okay with him, then it's okay with me.*

Jerry happily wagged his tail. At long last, he had a pet that was all his own.

PREDICT

How was this ending different from what you predicted? What might happen to Louisa now?

A Ghost of a Chance

There's nothing as intriguing— or as terrifying —as a haunted house on a dark night.

I tell you, that house is haunted!" Donny insisted, pointing to the house across the street from the graveyard.

Hal looked at his friend and rolled his eyes. "Give it up, Donny. You're <u>obsessed</u>."

"But I've seen lights going on and off, and heard sounds coming from inside."

"So why haven't I seen them?" asked Hal. "I tell you, the place is deserted."

"Then I dare you to spend the night there," Donny challenged.

"Fine," Hal replied, eager to prove he was right. And that evening Hal actually spent the night in the house that no other kid would have even dreamed of walking up to.

As soon as the sun went down, Hal quietly slipped through a window. It seemed to be a perfectly ordinary house . . . until he heard steps coming up the walk. He froze in terror. Suddenly he could hear two voices speaking to each other. They were just outside the front door! Hal panicked. He had to get out of there, but he was too afraid to move. What if they saw him? As the door swung open,

obsessed: unreasonably interested in

Hal clamped his hand over his mouth so he wouldn't let out a scream, and quietly watched from behind a curtain.

First a woman walked across the living room and lit two candles on the table. Then a man took dishes out of a cabinet and put them beside the candles. It seemed to Hal that they had done this before—as if they had done these things the same way, night after night, for who knows how long.

Feeling a little bolder, Hal moved closer to get a better look at the two of them. But as soon as he stepped out from behind the curtain, the woman looked directly at him, made an ugly face, and screamed. Hal screamed, too. Then the man made a horrible face at Hal and let out a wild shout.

Hal raced for the window and dove outside. He flew all the way back to the graveyard and over to where Donny was resting.

Donny took one look at Hal's white face. "You saw them, didn't you?"

"I sure did," Hal shivered. "They gave me the creeps."

"Well, I have to admit it, you're braver than I am," Donny said. "I'd never go among the living."

Hal floated slowly back to his grave. *They seemed almost as scared of me as I was of them,* he thought. And then, as his <u>insubstantial</u> form dissolved through the earth, he smiled wickedly. *Maybe,* he thought as he settled back into his coffin, *I'll visit them again.*

insubstantial: not real; imaginary

The Stray

▼ Learning from the Story

Work with a group of classmates. Have each person describe lunch time in your school cafeteria from a different perspective. Some suggestions might be

- a cafeteria worker
- a visiting parent
- the food

First make a list of words and phrases that describe the scene and events. Then write a paragraph or two. How does each person's or thing's past experiences affect how he, she, or it interprets the events?

▼ Putting It into Practice

Think about your own nightmarish story. Picture what's happening in your mind. Who (or what) is present besides you? Describe what's happening in your story to a partner. Have your partner take the part of the other person or thing and describe what's happening from that perspective. How does he, she, or it see the action differently?

NIGHT CRIES

Doesn't everyone know that a red sky in the morning means "sailor take warning"? Be warned!

Larry stood on a rise above the cold, wind-whipped seashore. Wave after foam-tipped wave rolled in from the steel-gray ocean and crashed on the rocky strip of beach below him. Larry had always loved the ocean. He was an excellent swimmer, and he'd taken sailing lessons for the past three summers. Something about the power of the sea and the loneliness of the shore reassured him. He felt as if he were standing at the edge of the earth. This was the perfect place to start a new life.

When Larry's mom died in a car accident eight months before, it seemed as if the whole world had been turned upside down. His dad tried to be strong and to help their relatives and friends through the grief and anger, but Larry soon realized that something in his father had died, too.

For a while, everyone tried to help and to be supportive. At first people were patient and understanding, but then things began to fall apart. Larry realized that his dad was becoming more and more withdrawn. He couldn't seem to concentrate, and his work suffered. Eventually, he lost his job, and they had to sell their house. Larry did everything he could to reach his father, but nothing seemed to work.

Then things suddenly began to take a turn for the better. Larry's dad had once been in the navy and he loved the sea, so when the job of lighthouse keeper at Bowman's Cove was offered to him by an old navy buddy, he jumped at the chance. Larry was pleased, too. They decided to start life over again as far away from their life in the city as possible. They had arrived in the seaside village three weeks ago, and the townspeople had welcomed them warmly. Larry had even made friends at his new school already.

Their new home was a small but cozy two-story cottage at the base of the lighthouse, which stood on a wide <u>jetty</u> known as Land's End. It deserved its lonely name. The jetty was a rugged mass of black rock that jutted out into the frigid Atlantic Ocean. A narrow, dangerous <u>channel</u> separated jagged Castle Rock from the point at the end of the jetty.

Larry took a deep breath of the crisp salt air and turned up the collar of his jacket against the autumn chill as he surveyed the scene. "It's absolutely perfect," he said aloud. His dog, Shah, wagged her tail in agreement. She, too, loved their early evening walks along the cove. Larry bent down and picked up a gnarly chunk of driftwood. Shah looked up expectantly.

"Go get it, girl," he shouted, tossing the wood with all his might. As the dog bounded across the sand, a flash of color drew Larry's attention to the rolling sea below the jetty. Straining to get a better look in the gathering dusk,

What details help you get a mental picture of Castle Rock and the lighthouse?

jetty: a structure built out into the water to protect a harbor

channel: a narrow body of water that connects two larger bodies of water

he caught a glimpse of a bright yellow slicker and the flutter of oars.

"Dad?" he said softly. "What in the world is he doing rowing out to Castle Rock now?"

"What, indeed?" The sound of a deep voice made Larry jump. A tall, burly man was sitting nearby on a jumble of rock.

"Joshua." Larry sighed with relief. "You startled me. I didn't see you there."

Shah raced up and dropped the driftwood at Larry's feet, then greeted the big fisherman happily. Shah liked Joshua. He had been very nice to Larry and his dad ever since they'd first arrived in Bowman's Cove. He and his wife had invited them to dinner at their home, and Joshua had even taken Larry for a boat tour of the local sites.

Joshua patted Shah on the head and glanced again toward the jetty. "This isn't a good time for anyone to be in these waters," he said with concern.

"I'm not worried," Larry said confidently. "Dad can handle a boat in any kind of weather. He must be rowing out to check the <u>buoys</u> in the channel. One of them broke loose last night." Still, Larry couldn't help being a little troubled. It was an odd time for his dad to be doing a chore like that.

"It isn't the sea that is to be feared, son," Joshua said. He tapped his pipe on the rock and then began to refill it with tobacco from an old leather pouch. "It's Sarah Malone." Joshua struck a match and held it to the bowl of the pipe.

buoys: floating markers that indicate safe waters

Larry studied the man's face for a moment in the flickering glow of the match light. "Okay," he said, grinning, "I'll bite. Who is Sarah Malone?"

"In life, she was a spiteful woman who did little good for most and seemed to go out of her way to be unpleasant," the fisherman began. "She didn't have a great many friends in Bowman's Cove. But in her defense, everyone said she was a devoted wife."

"Did you say in *life?*" Larry asked.

Joshua nodded. "That I did. Sarah Malone drew her last, tortured breath one hundred years ago, at the end of that very jetty." He tilted his head toward Castle Rock. "A powerful <u>gale</u> was blowing in from the northeast, and those that could brought their boats to port ahead of the fearsome storm. Colin Malone was said to have been a fine sailor, but the ocean is unpredictable. He never made it." Joshua paused to draw on his pipe. "Sarah would not accept that he was lost at sea. She came down to the shore herself that very night and crawled out onto the rocks. Screaming with rage and shaking her fists, she demanded that the ocean give her husband back."

"What happened to her?" Larry prompted.

"The sea claimed her as well," Joshua answered in a somber tone. "And since then, every quarter-century on the anniversary of her death, she returns to Castle Rock to seek <u>vengeance</u> by claiming another soul before the sun rises. Someone always drowns on that fateful night."

Larry laughed. "That's a great tale to scare tourists with, but you don't mean to tell me that the folks around here really believe it?"

gale: a very strong wind

vengeance: revenge

PREDICT

Why do you think the author included this legend? What do you think will happen in the story?

The look on Joshua's face made Larry's smile fade. "I do," Joshua said, gazing out at the waves. "You won't see a ship from Bowman's Cove leaving the harbor on this day or the next. The time is only two nights away, and Sarah might already be working her evil enchantment. She chooses her victim carefully and sways his thoughts." Joshua leaned closer to Larry as if to tell him something of great importance. "You'll find all of the local fishermen safely at home in front of a warm fire, with the shutters secured across the windows to close out the sound of the sea."

From high above, Larry heard the strange, eerie call of a large seabird circling through the mist overhead. "That's the great northern diver," Joshua said solemnly. "Its arrival is another sign that the time is near. The bird is waiting . . . hoping to rescue the unfortunate soul from Sarah Malone's grasp and escort the phantom into eternity."

Later, at home in his warm bed, Larry couldn't fall asleep. Usually he found the sound of the waves soothing, but tonight was different. He hadn't really believed the old legend that Joshua had told him, but now something about the ocean sounded sinister. After tossing and turning for a while, he stood and looked out of his bedroom window. The water shimmered with reflected moonlight, and the dark jetty stood out sharply. Larry studied the stark outline of Castle Rock and watched the angry sea foaming around the rocks that lurked just beneath the surface. Then he saw something else. Huddling beside him, Shah nudged gently at his hand and whimpered.

"Do you see it, too, girl?" Larry whispered. "It looks like . . ." Larry's eyes widened and he tried to make sense of what he was looking at. "There's someone standing on Castle Rock. That's impossible! How could anyone . . . ?"

The words died in his throat. For a moment, Larry clearly glimpsed the form of a young woman. Her long hair and flowing white gown danced on the wind. Then, before his eyes, she seemed to fade into a wispy haze.

"I don't believe it," he said firmly to himself. "It was just sea foam or fog or something. Now old Joshua's got me seeing things." Shaking his head, Larry dropped his gaze to the beach below and caught his breath. There was his father, standing on the beach in his pajamas. He was staring in the direction of the point . . . as if in a trance.

✳ ✳ ✳

Larry was up early the next morning. He noticed that the sky on the horizon was a deep shade of red.

"Red sky in the morning, sailor take warning," he recited to Shah. "We'll probably be getting a pretty bad storm soon." Larry knew there was some truth to that old saying. It had something to do with moisture in the air and how it reflected sunlight. He dressed quickly and marched downstairs. It was Saturday, and he and his dad always drove into town on Saturday for a special pancake breakfast at the diner. He found his dad in the kitchen preparing toast and hot cereal.

"What's up, Dad?" Larry asked. "Aren't we going to town for breakfast?"

His father grinned and set a plate of toast on the table, then turned back to the stove. He seemed to be in a great mood. "I have a lot of work to catch up on around here, son. Would you mind terribly if we skipped it today?"

PREDICT

Do you want to change your prediction? What do you think will happen to Larry's father?

Larry tried to hide his disappointment. "I guess not," he murmured, picking up a triangle of buttery toast. "Dad, did you see it, too?"

"See what?" his father asked.

Larry could tell that something was <u>amiss</u>. "I know it sounds really crazy, but I was sure I saw a woman out on Castle Rock last night. I thought maybe the reason you went outside was because you'd seen her, too."

His father stiffened slightly, and his mood seemed to darken. "I wasn't outside last night," he answered. "You must have been dreaming."

"But, Dad, I—"

"You must have been dreaming," his dad repeated, sternly. "Sit down and eat your breakfast before it gets cold. I have to see to some things outside."

Larry flinched as the kitchen door banged shut. Glancing down, he noticed his father's slippers on the floor near the door. He picked them up and ran his finger across the toes. They were damp and covered with sand.

✳ ✳ ✳

That night, the weather took a turn for the worse. Snug in his bed, Larry suddenly awakened and listened as the howl of the wind rose outside and rattled the window panes. He squeezed his eyes tightly shut. He wanted to stay right where he was . . . safe from whatever terror was building out there in the dark. But somehow he felt himself being drawn to the window. Slowly, he pushed the blankets aside and went to the window. He stood looking out at the seething ocean. This time, he could see the woman clearly. She raised her hand and seemed to beckon him.

Why did Larry's father deny being outside last night?

amiss: wrong; not normal

"Sarah Malone," Larry whispered under his breath. But all at once he became aware that it wasn't *he* that she wanted. A sense of panic gripped him. Larry looked down and frantically scanned the beach. Stunned, he saw his father untying one of the small boats secured at the dock. He threw open his window and screamed out into the tumultuous night.

"Dad! No!" But the icy wind stung Larry's face and whipped his warning away. His father jumped into the craft and headed out into the rough water. Fighting his own terror, Larry threw on his clothes and sprinted to the dock.

He worked to untie the second boat. Sea spray had soaked the knots and made them difficult to untie, but finally Larry freed the boat. He leapt into it and began to row with all his might. The ocean roared in protest, and he strained at the oars to make headway against the rolling swells. Twisting to look over his shoulder, he could see Sarah Malone standing like a ghastly sentinel on Castle Rock. Her eyes blazed red, and she threw back her head in ghostly laughter as Larry's dad allowed his boat to become caught in the swirling waves around the rock. Drawing nearer to the point, Larry heard snatches of his father's voice carried on the wind.

"Anna!" he cried out above the clamor of the surge. "Don't leave me again!"

"No!" Larry screamed. "She's tricked you, Dad. That isn't Mom—it's Sarah Malone!" But it was too late. In horror, Larry watched his father's boat enveloped by a veil of foam and dragged beneath the surface.

tumultuous: stormy; rough

surge: a series of rolling waves

enveloped: covered

"No, Sarah Malone!" Larry howled defiantly. "I won't let you win!"

The spiteful phantom turned her eyes on the terrified boy, and the oars flew from his hands. Suddenly trapped in the churning surge, the small boat began to splinter beneath Larry. He was thrown into the icy black water.

"DAD!" he screamed, choking and gasping for breath. "DAD! HELP ME!"

Suddenly, Larry felt his head being held safely above the surface. He saw the sky begin to lighten with the first glimmer of sunrise. He also sensed his father's strong arms around him and heard his voice. But he couldn't actually feel his father's physical presence.

"Hang on, son!" His father's voice was strange and distant. "You'll make it!"

The dawn was growing brighter as Larry felt firm sand beneath him and dragged himself onto shore. "We did it, Dad!" he gasped, thinking his father was right beside him. "This time she didn't win."

His father's answer seemed to be coming from far away. "No, this time she didn't win. She turned her attention to you for only a moment, but it was long enough to free me . . . to save you."

Larry sat up shivering. He was alone on the beach. He stared out at the point and saw nothing but waves crashing against the barren rock. Then, from above, he heard the eerie call of the great northern diver as it began its journey. Sarah Malone had lost her battle to capture their souls, but Larry knew that he had lost, too. His father was gone forever.

PREDICT

Were your predictions correct so far? What do you think will happen to Larry now?

▼ Learning from the Story

Although you've never been to Bowman's Cove, you have a pretty good idea what it looks like—thanks to the author's vivid description of the setting. Can you do as good a job? Play "Where Am I?" with several other students.

1. Pick a place that everyone should know.
2. Describe the location. Use vivid words and phrases that help people get a mental picture of exactly what the place is like.
3. Continue until someone in your group can identify the place.
4. List on the board the words and phrases that were most helpful in narrowing down the location.

▼ Putting It into Practice

Take photos or make sketches of places in your town that might make the perfect setting for your nightmarish story. Show the setting during the day and at night, if you can. Also show it from several angles. Keep these photos or drawings in your story file and pull them out whenever you need to describe the setting.

Seeing is not always believing.

The Last Wave

Or should that be the other way around?

Ryan Mitchell squats on the smooth pebbles of Hideaway Beach and watches his older brother, Todd, walk into the waist-high surf of Half-Moon Bay. Todd wades past the small waves and slaps his surfboard onto the murky, gray-green water. Then he slides belly-first onto the board and paddles through the foamy swells toward the bigger waves a hundred yards out.

As he watches Todd thrust his wet-suited arms shoulder-deep into the salty water, effortlessly gliding the fluorescent green board through the chilly bay, Ryan admires the strength and power in his brother's stroke. *Will my arms and back ever be that strong?* Ryan wonders. He can't even imagine ever being as lean and athletic as Todd—at eighteen, already the best surfer Half-Moon Bay has ever known.

The bright sunlight bouncing off the waves forces Ryan to squint as he follows his brother's path into deeper water. He shades his eyes and sees that Todd has reached the next line of waves at the <u>inlet</u> where large, eight-foot crests break into smaller pieces and run to the beach. Todd is now sitting upright on his board, rising and falling in the

inlet: a bay

swelling water like a fishing bobber, waiting for the perfect wave to carry him back to the <u>shallows</u>.

Listening to sea lions honk on the dark, jagged ledges and jutting rocks that ring the tiny strip of beach, Ryan imagines himself out there, impressing all the girls. *Well, maybe when I'm bulked up a little,* he thinks. *Maybe when I'm a little more like Todd.*

Half-Moon Bay, Ryan knows, is a tough spot to surf. The water is practically frigid, and the tide running out of the narrow, crescent-shaped bay could carry an inexperienced surfer halfway to Santa Cruz. Also, sharks come into the bay, swimming very close to shore, where their favorite food—sea lions—come each spring to mate and have pups. Ryan has heard dozens of stories of bitten boards and of sharks mistaking surfers for seals. In fact, the stories are told like legends among the surfing crowd, but they always make Ryan shudder.

As one of the horrible stories pops into his mind, Ryan's thoughts are suddenly broken by the flash of Todd's vivid green surfboard shooting to the water's surface. Grabbing his high-powered binoculars, Ryan leaps up to get a better look at his brother, who has caught a huge wave.

His body crouched, Todd centers his weight as the swelling water lifts and propels him shoreward. Ryan watches in awe as the ocean rises behind Todd and carries him in its huge, watery palm.

But all of a sudden, Todd banks right and the board noses up and over the white froth. Like a cowboy jumping into the saddle, Ryan's show-off brother has straddled his

shallows: an area where the water is not very deep

board and now raises his arm skyward, twirling an imaginary lariat. "Darn you, Todd," Ryan mutters under his breath, as he realizes his brother is just goofing around. "What a ham."

"*Yeeee-haw! Yeeeeeee-haw!*" Todd's deep voice cuts through the crashing surf. He shakes his long blond hair out of his eyes and waves at Ryan, who waves back.

In the bright sunlight, Ryan can hardly see the stump where Todd's arm ends just above the wrist. The wet suit covers his other scars, so anyone else on the beach would see only a free-spirited surfer. But Ryan remembers the ribbons of flesh, the torn tissue, and the splintered bone that were once his brother's body. Ryan remembers the terrible hulking shape rising from the murky waters, the gushing fountains of blood, and the throat-ripping screams of pain that rose from his brother's throat. It's amazing Todd's alive, let alone surfing again . . . out there.

How does this description of Todd's accident make you feel? What do you think the author had in mind? ▶

❋ ❋ ❋

It had happened not even a full two years ago, in spring, when seal <u>rookeries</u> were filled with crying pups, and <u>cows</u> spent their days trying to keep their young fed. The rocks around Half-Moon Bay practically glistened from the fur of thousands of the sleek, barking seals, and macho <u>bulls</u> made all kinds of noise fighting over their mates.

Todd had outfitted his van for a camping and surfing weekend. A rack for boards had been bolted onto the roof, and the floor had been covered with foam padding, just right for sacking out on. He'd even bought a propane lantern and stove, and the huge cooler was stocked with every kind of soda, not to mention enormous submarine sandwiches.

rookeries: nests or breeding grounds

cows: female seals

bulls: male seals

Todd and his buddies were going to the perfect surfer's escape at Hideaway Beach. With its rocky shore and bone-chilling water, Hideaway kept the swimsuit crowd away. Only a few kids at school even knew about it, and it had become like a private surfers' club.

Ryan could hardly believe it when Todd had asked him to come along—and his parents had said okay. The brothers had always been pretty tight, even though Todd was four years older. But Ryan never dreamed he'd be hanging out and surfing with the coolest guys in school.

Actually, Ryan wasn't much of a surfer. He liked the ocean, and he knew a lot more than most kids about marine life, but he'd never been able to catch a wave and ride a <u>curl</u> like Todd and the older guys. Ryan just wasn't very athletic, nor was he very strong. His knees wobbled every time he tried to move on the board to steer it, and he fell more often than not. The truth was, Ryan was more interested in what was happening *under* the waves than on top of them, and he knew that Todd had only invited him to tag along to psych him up about surfing. "You've just got to center your mind and body," Todd would always say. "You've got to be lifted by the power of the ocean."

The only problem was that the ocean didn't cooperate that day. The weather had been perfect, all right—sunny and clear, with a breeze blowing down from the Santa Cruz mountains—but the waves were tiny, choppy, and totally useless to a surfer. Todd and his buddies waited, their wet suits zipped, their surfboards bobbing like corks in the gentle <u>heaves</u>, but the breeze kept the surf down,

curl: the hollow arch of water formed by a breaking wave

heaves: rising and falling motions

and by Sunday morning most of the campers had packed up their boards and headed home.

But not Todd. He had been determined to surf and determined to show his little brother how to ride the waves. "I'm not leaving until I get the waves I came here for," he'd told Ryan. "We're going to surf together if it's the last thing I do."

Ryan had wanted to go home—not because he'd given up on surfing, but because he was afraid. On an early morning walk along the beach, he'd seen a large brown lump at the foot of the rocky cliffs. As he'd gotten closer, he'd seen a buzzing cloud of green flies rising over what he'd soon come to realize was the smelly remains of an enormous sea lion—a bull, probably ten feet long. Actually, it was hard to tell how big the animal had been, because only the top half of the carcass—from just below the first flipper up to the snout—had washed up on the beach. Below the fins, a gooey, purplish mass of blubber and guts wriggling with maggots spilled onto the dark sand, and Ryan felt his stomach <u>heave</u>. He knew right away what had happened. Something had bitten the sea lion completely in half.

Todd had just shrugged when Ryan told him about the mangled carcass. "Probably got run over by a boat," he'd said. "Come on. Let's paddle out past the point. The breeze is really coming off the water today."

Ryan knew that a boat couldn't cut a sea lion in half—chew it up, maybe; take chunks from its flesh, sure; but it couldn't slice through hundreds of pounds of fat and sever

heave: to make an effort to vomit

a spinal cord. Only one thing could do that, and it wasn't an engine—it had to be an eating machine . . . like a great white shark.

Still, somehow Todd had convinced him to go, and with his teeth chattering, Ryan paddled out toward the deeper water, just barely keeping up with Todd's powerful strokes. It was a warm day, but the fear that had passed through Ryan's bones at the sight of the mangled animal had left a tremor in his body that he could not control.

Finally, Todd had stopped paddling and straddled his board almost a hundred yards from the beach. Ryan pulled up next to him and remained belly-first on the board as he positioned it toward shore. *Please let a good wave come quickly*, he'd thought, *so Todd can get this out of his system and we can go home.* But the murky, greenish-gray water simply rose and fell like a giant's soft breathing, gently lifting and lowering their boards.

Thwack! Thwack!

Ryan winced, remembering how Todd had slammed the water in frustration. "I'll just have to make my own waves!" his feisty brother had yelled.

Ryan had looked over at Todd nervously. "I don't think it's such a good idea to do that. You never know what's down there. Sometimes sharks—"

"Get off this shark thing, Ryan!" Todd had snapped, looking at Ryan like he was a total wimp. "More people get hit by lightning every year than get bitten by sharks."

If you were Ryan, would you have gone surfing? Why or why not?

That's because people stay inside during thunderstorms—they don't go looking for lightning, Ryan had thought. In fact, he would remember thinking that for the rest of his life.

Thwack! Thwack!

Todd had slapped the water again, as if taunting the ocean to cooperate. "I'm not quitting," he'd told Ryan. "If you want to paddle in, go ahead. I'm waiting for the waves."

And so Todd had turned his board toward deeper waters. "I'll see you later, chicken," he'd said, raising his arm to wave.

Ryan had seen the shark hit before Todd had even lowered his arm. The water seemed to boil around his brother's board as the huge gray shape rose from the bottom and hit like a runaway train—a train with jaws like two monstrous chain saws.

Once again Ryan winced, remembering how Todd's feet had suddenly pointed to the sky as the creature flipped him and began to drag him under. And, oh, how Todd had fought! He'd battled to the surface several times and had even looked at Ryan, his mouth forming a distorted oval as he'd screamed in shock and terror. Then, without warning, Todd had vanished, yanked below to the ocean depths with his arms flailing like a rag doll, the churning waters turning a hideous red.

And what had *he* done? Ryan now thought with a sick feeling rising in his stomach. He'd frozen, but not before a cool wave of vomit had risen from his stomach. Sure, he'd finally fought off every urge in his body to flee; and yes,

PREDICT

What do you think happens to Todd? What details make you think this?

he'd finally forced himself to paddle toward the bloody, foaming water twenty yards away. But then he'd frozen again when he'd seen Todd rise from the water, the upper half of his body zooming along the surface, while the lower half remained tight in the shark's hideous grip.

It was all still so clear in Ryan's memory. In that frozen moment, he'd seen the white stripes of his brother's splintered ribs through his shredded wet suit. And he'd seen how Todd had reached out to him, grunting in pain, unable even to scream because the air had been driven from his lungs. And how could Ryan ever forget how he'd given a quick thrust with his board so he could reach out for Todd's hand . . . which came off above the wrist, leaving only shattered bone and gory ribbons of tissue at the end of the arm.

"No!" Ryan had screamed, his eyes wide in horror as he saw the huge gray shape rising from the dark background to claim another piece of Todd. Then, with a violent scream that rose from the core of his body, Ryan had kicked out at the shark's snout, hoping to distract it away from his brother.

But suddenly, it was *he* who had felt a <u>searing</u> pain. For when he had kicked at the shark, his leg had driven into the huge cavern that was the shark's mouth. Ryan remembered looking straight down at the beast's triangular teeth set in rows, like thousands of three-inch bayonets.

"No! No! No!" he'd screamed over and over, each time hammering the shark's mouth with every ounce of strength he had. Pain had rushed through him as the monster's rough scales tore into his wet flesh, but the last

searing: burning

Which image on this page is the most powerful? Explain why you think as you do.

blow had definitely loosened its hold on his leg, and Ryan had pulled free.

"Todd!" he'd yelled, as the terrible shark sank beneath the waves again.

And then Ryan had spotted him. Only about five feet away, there was Todd, thrashing in the darkening water, trying somehow to swim from the agony. Making a desperate lunge for his brother, Ryan had managed to get his fingers on a torn flap of Todd's wet suit. Then, just before Todd sank beneath the water, Ryan had hauled his mangled body out of the surf and had placed his arm across Todd's groaning chest in a lifeguard's carry. Paddling with his free arm, praying out loud that the shark had left to look for other prey, Ryan had headed to shore.

After what had seemed like a lifetime, Ryan's feet had finally touched sand, and he'd dragged his brother's torn body onto the beach. Exhausted, still in shock himself, he'd crawled over to the towels they had left only a half-hour earlier, wrapped one around the gushing wound on his own leg, and then scrambled back to Todd with the other.

Covered with so much blood that it was impossible to see his wounds, Todd had lain nearly lifeless on the beach. Ryan had gently put the towel over his brother and knelt by his side. Placing his left hand on Todd's ribs to hold them in place, he'd begun mouth-to-mouth <u>resuscitation</u> when, like a godsend, a helicopter had appeared in the distance.

✳ ✳ ✳

resuscitation: the act of reviving from unconsciousness

Mrs. Mitchell waits in the driveway as Ryan pulls the van in. "Ryan! Where have you been?" she asks impatiently. "Dad and I have been worried sick!"

Ryan smiles. "I was at Hideaway, Mom."

"You *drove* all the way to Hideaway?" Mrs. Mitchell sputters. "You can't drive that far yet, honey. You *know* that."

Ryan slides awkwardly out of the driver's seat. His eyes shine happily. "I saw Todd, Mom. I saw him there."

Mrs. Mitchell looks at the ground and shakes her head. She looks back up at her son, with tears streaming down her face. "Ryan, honey, we've been going to Dr. Bransfield to talk about this for two years now."

"But Mom, Todd was—"

"No, Ryan. Todd *wasn't*. Todd is dead."

"But I saved him, Mom!" Ryan's voice rises in panic. "I pulled him to the beach. I covered him with—"

"No, Ryan. We never found Todd. You know that. We talk about this each week with the doctor." Mrs. Mitchell sighs. "When the fishermen found you, you had almost bled to death yourself. Remember, honey?"

Ryan begins to cry. "Yes . . . yes, I remember."

"And what did you have, Ryan?" Mrs. Mitchell asks gently.

"Todd's hand," he whispers. "I—I had Todd's hand in my hand."

Ryan looks at the ground. His shoulders heave and tears run off his nose, splashing on the plastic limb just below his knee to his shoe.

"Come on, honey." Mrs. Mitchell puts her arm around Ryan's waist. "Let's go inside. Don't cry. Once you learn how to use that leg a little better, you can drive anyplace you want—even to Hideaway."

How was this ending different from your prediction?

The Last Wave

▼ Learning from the Story

"The Last Wave" brings dozens of images to mind—of frothy green seas and gruesome mangled bodies. Can you paint images in someone's mind, too?

Look through a magazine for an interesting photo of a person or place. Work with a partner to list as many words and phrases as you can to describe the photo. Be sure your words create mental images and appeal to the five senses. Compare your list with other students' lists. Which group was able to paint the most vivid images in your mind?

▼ Putting It into Practice

Take the photo or drawing of you facing your worst fear from your story file. Make a list of words that describe what you're thinking and feeling in that photo. What do you smell, feel, see, hear, or taste? Write these sensory images on a note card. Weave some of these descriptions into your story. Can you make your readers actually feel as if they are experiencing *your* worst nightmare?

CAR FOUR

It began when they redecorated my father's office building. The lobby used to be warm and friendly, with a big vase of dried flowers on an oak table surrounded by soft, comfortable chairs. When they redecorated, all this was replaced by stiff, black leather chairs and an ugly chrome table. The walls were now unpainted concrete, as if the building were still under construction, and icy blue lights threw patterns of shadow on the wall. It all looked very trendy, but to me it just felt cold. *Who would want to work here?* I thought, wishing things didn't always have to change.

My brother and I both got the chills as we walked into that stark, unpleasant lobby. Markie grabbed my hand tightly as we stepped up to the security guard.

"Marissa, this isn't Dad's building," said Markie.

"Don't be dumb. Of course it is," I said like a stern older sister.

Even the security guard was new—a pale-looking man with sunken cheeks, and eyes the same color as the concrete walls. Behind him a giant gunmetal-gray clock that looked like a gear in some terrible factory sliced the hour into

What goes up must come down— most of the time.

What feeling do you get from the description of the building and the guard? What mood is the author creating?

minutes with steely hands as sharp as knives. The grim guard stared at us coldly, as if we were trespassing on a grave.

"May I help you?" he asked.

I sighed and went through the speech as quickly as possible. "We're Markie and Marissa Hernandez. Our father is Carlos Hernandez, of Hernandez and Stevens, Attorneys at Law. Our mom *always* drops us off every Friday at five so we can spend the weekend with our father."

"They're divorced," said Markie, whispering it like it was a big terrible disease.

The gloomy guard nodded and sent us on our way. We headed toward the elevator banks, our sneakers squeaking on the gray marble floor.

Even the elevators had changed; the wood-paneled doors were now shiny, mirrored steel.

As we approached the elevator bank, Markie clutched his stuffed elephant to his chest and took a deep breath, a routine he repeated whenever we got near an elevator.

I guess most kids love elevators, especially fast ones that make you feel heavy on the way up and tingly light on the way down. Not Markie, though. Markie hates elevators.

When he was four, we were in an elevator at the mall—a stupid elevator, really, since the mall only had two floors and the elevator moved so slowly you could climb the stairs faster. Still, Markie and I wanted to ride the elevator, so Mom, Dad, Markie, and I got in. But just as the door was closing, Markie saw that he had dropped his teddy bear just outside of the elevator car. As he grabbed it, the door closed on his hand and slowly began to rise to the second floor.

It was awful. Mom began to scream, and both she and Dad, in a panic, fought to pry the elevator doors open. But they wouldn't budge. Markie began to howl as my parents started tugging on his arm. They were looking at his arm, but I was looking at his eyes, and I knew the moment it happened. It was the moment his pupils went wide. He gasped, and in that second, his face became <u>mottled</u> purple and red, and he screamed like I never heard anyone scream before.

Finally, after what seemed like an eternity, the elevator reached the second floor. The bell dinged cheerfully, and the doors pulled apart as if nothing had happened.

The people waiting outside the elevator were the first to see it. They saw a screaming boy gripping the severed leg of a teddy bear, his own bloody hand missing a <u>pinky</u>.

Mom and Dad blamed each other for that and lots of other things, and eventually got divorced. Dad, being a hotshot lawyer, filed a lawsuit against the mall and won enough money to put Markie and me through college someday. I never knew a pinky could be worth so much money.

The accident was three years ago, but to Markie it might as well have been yesterday.

Now he clutched the stuffed elephant that had replaced his ruined teddy bear, practically strangling the thing as we approached the new mirrored doors of the elevator bank in Dad's office building. Markie walked slowly and fearfully, just as he had when we went to Nana's funeral last year.

PREDICT

Why do you think the author included this incident? How might this foreshadow what will happen?

mottled: marked with spots or blotches

pinky: the little finger

Three of the four elevators were out of service, leaving only one car—car four—to carry people to the building's thirty floors.

"Mechanical problems," I said, reading the sign for Markie.

"What kind of mechanical problems?" he asked.

I considered making up a story about how someone was cut in half, but decided against it. "They probably just need to grease the gears or something," I told him.

Finally car four arrived, and a wave of people came flowing out like sardines from a can, and smelling just as bad. When the car was empty, people forced their way in ahead of us, and Markie and I barely squeezed into the car.

The inside of the elevator used to be paneled wood, but now the walls and ceiling were mirrored glass, making the small, crowded elevator seem like an immense hall packed with a thousand people trapped deep within the glass. The mirrored walls reflected each other over and over, sending light ping-ponging back and forth in the little box of a room, like a fun house where no one was having fun.

How does the author describe the elevator?

The elevator door slammed behind Markie, and as the elevator rose, my ears began to pop. That's when I noticed that Markie, standing with his back up against the door, was sobbing silently to himself.

"Markie, are you okay?"

"It's eating me," he whispered through his tears.

"What?"

"The elevator is eating me." He was terrified, and his face was turning that awful shade of purple. When

I looked behind him, I saw that the right cheek of his behind was firmly pinched between the steel elevator doors.

"Help me," he whimpered.

Other people began to notice and tried to help, but the doors would not open a fraction of an inch. Markie sobbed until the door finally opened, and car four released him from its steel jaws.

Once we were in Dad's office, it took half an hour to calm Markie down. Dad examined his rear to find a thin red welt, as if Markie had been pinched in a <u>vise</u>. To make things worse, somewhere between the first and twenty-third floors Markie had managed to lose his little stuffed elephant. He swore that the elevator ate it.

On the way down to the lobby, Dad had to hold Markie in his arms. Markie clung to him, holding his breath and squeezing his eyes shut.

There were just the three of us in the elevator, and I quickly realized how terrible car four truly was. With nothing but mirrors everywhere, all I could see was a thousand reflections of us stretching in all directions toward a dim, gray <u>infinity</u>. All I could hear was the wind whistling in the shaft. All I could smell was an awful aroma of the new gray carpet beneath my feet. I have to admit, I closed my eyes and began to hold my breath long before we reached the lobby.

The following Friday, Mom dropped us off at the steps of Dad's office building as she always did. "Can't you come up with us?" begged Markie.

vise: a tool with two jaws that close and are used to hold an object in place

infinity: unlimited, endless space

"It's not a good idea," said Mom, which was her nice way of saying that she never wanted to see Dad again for as long as she lived.

"Please . . ." Markie pleaded.

"Markie," said Mom, "it only takes you a minute to get to his office."

"A minute is a long way," said Markie.

Mom unfastened his seat belt for him and stuffed a brand-new teddy bear into his arms. "It's okay, honey," she said. "Marissa will protect you."

I hated her for that.

We climbed the steps toward the tower, nearing the revolving doors that spun like propellers, sucking people in and spitting people out.

"Sometimes," said Markie, "sometimes I'm afraid I'll get lost between Mom and Dad."

"Don't be silly," I told him, but I knew exactly how he felt. It was like last year when I flew out alone to visit Aunt Lita. There's no lonelier moment in the universe than the moment between your family and the plane. There's a long hallway you have to go through after you've said goodbye to your mom before the stewardess finally greets you at the plane's hatch. That hallway has to be the longest, most awful hallway in the world—and that's how the trip from Mom's car to Dad's office must have felt to Markie.

Together we let ourselves be sucked into the revolving doors and spat out into the <u>bleak</u> lobby.

PREDICT

Now that you have read the descriptions of the elevator and Markie's fear, what do you think might happen?

bleak: dull and depressing

We waited in silence at the elevator banks. All four elevators were working, but car four was the first one to arrive.

"No!" Markie held me back, so we waited for the next elevator. Car four came back before any of the others.

Markie stood back and we waited once more. Two minutes passed, and at last an elevator came. Car four, again.

This time I felt so stupid about it that I made Markie get into the crowded elevator, figuring all the others were just tied up on high floors. I pushed Markie in first, making sure I was between him and the closing doors.

Then the elevator started to move.

Down.

Markie gasped, and so did I. I know this is dumb, but there's something truly terrifying about getting in an elevator and feeling it go in the wrong direction. Sure, what goes down has to come back up, but for that tiny split second before your brain makes sense of what's going on, all you can feel is the sudden panic that something's gone wrong. Even when your brain kicks in a moment later, some of that feeling stays with you.

The elevator emptied out on the underground parking levels, leaving Markie and me to ride up alone. With the elevator empty, Markie pushed himself up against the back wall, as far away from the doors as he could get. He plastered himself against the mirrored wall, gripping his new teddy bear, which didn't seem to give him any of the comfort his little stuffed elephant had given him.

How do the author's descriptions and word choice help to set the mood and build suspense?

PREDICT

Can Marissa protect Markie? Will what happens to him be good or bad? What details make you think as you do?

kaleidoscope: a tube containing loose bits of colored glass or plastic between two flat plates and with two mirrors that reflect changes of the position of the colored material to form endless patterns

Marissa will protect you. Mom's words rang in my ears. I wished she had never given that responsibility to me.

I pushed 23—Dad's floor—and watched as the numbers began to climb. My ears started to pop and I tried to avoid looking at the thousand reflections of myself in the mirrors around me. No one else got in.

"See, Markie?" I said, turning to him. "There's nothing to worry about . . ." That's when I realized that I wasn't looking at Markie at all; I was looking at one of his reflections in the mirror. I turned to look the other way.

"Markie?"

I reached to touch him, but my hand fell upon cold glass.

I spun around. Markie was nowhere . . . and everywhere! There were a hundred reflections of him, but that's all they were—*reflections.* I reached to all the walls, desperately touching them with my fingertips, but Markie was not in the elevator! It was as if he had somehow slipped into the mirrors and was lost somewhere *inside* them.

"Marissa?" Markie began to move, and his thousand reflections shifted like a human kaleidoscope. I could see him in the mirrors, reaching toward my reflections, trying to find the real me, the same way I was trying to find the real him. He began to cry. "Marissa, where are you?" He turned and headed deeper into the maze of reflections, getting farther and farther away.

"Marissa?!" he screamed, panicking now, trapped. I saw his many reflections run deeper into the mirrors, getting smaller and smaller.

"Marissa!" he screamed more frantically. "Where are you? Don't leave me all alone!"

"Markie!" I screamed back. "No!" But he couldn't hear me anymore. All I could do was scream and press my hands against the cold glass, watching as my little brother went deeper and deeper into the mirrors—until he was just a shadow that disappeared into the dark distance. Soon, his voice faded into the whistling wind racing through the elevator shaft, and there was nothing left around me but my own reflections, stretching in all directions forever and ever and ever.

The bell dinged cheerfully, and the elevator doors opened.

"Marissa?" It was my father, who must have heard me screaming. In tears I raced out of the elevator into his arms.

"Honey, what's wrong? Where's Markie?"

"He's gone, Daddy," I wailed. "Markie's gone!"

"What do you mean, *gone*?"

And then my dad noticed something that I didn't. Lying there in the corner of the elevator was Markie's stuffed elephant, the one that had vanished in the elevator the week before.

"Markie?" Just as Dad reached into the elevator, the door closed on his arm, all the way up to his shoulder.

"Daddy, no!" I shrieked.

People yelled and tried to pry him free, but all I could do was watch my father's eyes as car four began its return trip to the lobby.

PREDICT

Is this story going to have a happy ending? What do you think will happen? Why?

▼ Learning from the Story

Writers use setting, lighting, and words to create a mood. Music can also set the mood. Look back over "Car Four." What kind of elevator music would you pick to play inside car four? Work with several other students to choose a piece of music that matches the cold decor of the elevator and also hints at events that will happen there.

▼ Putting It into Practice

When you record your story, you'll have to create a mood using words and sounds alone. Background music can help create that mood, too. Listen to tapes and CDs to find one that will create just the right mood for your story. Instrumentals usually work best for background music. Once you've found just the right piece, try it out. Read your nightmarish story as the music plays in the background. Why does the combination work? What words describe the mood the music creates?

GROWING PAINS

The scream stabbed into Cody Fenchurch's sleep, tearing a jagged hole in his dream. He had been dreaming he was tall—the tallest kid in school—towering over all the other kids who always teased him about his height. But great dreams like that never last, and Cody was dragged away from that happy fantasy into the cold darkness of his room. He sat up, blinking in the moonlight, wondering who had screamed—and why.

Suddenly a second scream rattled his half-opened window, and Cody knew that both screams had come from next door. That's where his best friend, Warren Burke, lived.

Cody stared through his large window and could see right into Warren's room. He could see his friend sitting in bed and wailing. What was happening in there? It sounded like Warren was being torn to pieces.

Cody watched as the lights came on next door and Warren's parents raced into his room. By then, Warren was running around, waving and thrashing his arms at empty air.

Soon Cody realized that his own parents were awake, too. He heard them whispering down the hall, talking about what was going on at the neighbor's house, and

It hurts to be the shortest kid in class. But you have no idea how painful it is being the tallest!

wondering what to do. Then his dad poked his head into Cody's room. "You okay, sport?" he asked.

Cody assured his dad that he was, then he tried to go back to sleep. That's when Warren screamed again, and this time Cody heard him say something, too.

"Don't let them come back!" Warren shrieked. "Don't let them take me again! It's horrible! Horrible!"

Cody listened to Warren's mad ravings, and then he listened to Mr. and Mrs. Burke trying to calm him down. "It's only a dream," they kept telling him over and over again.

But that didn't seem to calm Warren down in the least. In fact, he continued to scream the rest of that awful, endless night, and Cody slept—or tried to sleep—with a pillow over his head.

In the morning, Warren was still screaming. And he was still screaming that next afternoon . . . when he was taken off to the hospital. As far as Cody knew, Warren never did stop screaming.

And that's how Cody Fenchurch lost his best friend.

PREDICT

Why was Warren screaming all night?

❊ ❊ ❊

"But you have to *try* to sleep," Cody's mom insisted. It had been three weeks since Warren Burke had been taken away, and once again, here Cody was, lying on his bed, his eyes wide open.

"You know what they say," his mother offered. "You grow when you sleep."

"I'm trying," said Cody, rolling over restlessly. "I always try."

His mother raised an eyebrow. "You're thinking about Warren, aren't you?"

"No," Cody said flatly. It was a lie, of course. How could he not think about Warren? He thought about him every time he looked out his window and saw his friend's empty room across the way. He thought about him every time he walked home from school—alone.

"Would you like to visit Warren?" Cody's mom asked.

Cody sat up in bed. "You mean they let kids visit other kids in the <u>asylum</u>?"

She wrinkled her nose, as if the word *asylum* had a stench to it. "They don't call those places asylums anymore, Cody," she informed him. "They're just hospitals—*special* hospitals."

Cody thought about that and looked out the window toward Warren's dark, empty room. For years he and Warren had talked to each other at night across the narrow pathway between their two houses, about all sorts of things—school, girls, sports—and growing up.

Growing up.

That had been a sore point with Cody. He and Warren had always been about the same height until fifth grade. But then Warren had started having what they called "growth spurts." One summer he even grew two whole inches.

But Cody didn't have any growth spurts. In fact, he hadn't grown a fraction of an inch in two years. While all the other kids in school were sprouting long, clumsy arms and legs, Cody remained unchanged.

asylum: a hospital for the insane

Now, in the middle of seventh grade, Cody was the shortest kid in the class, and Warren, if he hadn't been locked away somewhere, would have been the tallest. Cody remembered how ridiculous he used to feel walking home next to Warren. But Warren had never made fun of Cody's size—not like the other kids. That's why they had been able to stay best friends.

So now that his best friend had gone insane and had been taken away, did Cody want to visit him? Did he *really* want to visit Warren after he had heard him scream for twelve straight hours?

Cody looked at his mom, who was standing at the edge of his bed. "Is it true that Warren's hair turned white that night?" he blurted out.

His mother offered him a slim smile and said wistfully, "That happens sometimes."

❋ ❋ ❋

Harmony Home for Children did its best to be pleasant and inviting, but the <u>disinfectant</u>-scented linoleum couldn't hide the smell of decay, and the music pumped into the air couldn't hide the sounds of madness.

Warren was in a room at the end of a long hallway papered with balloons and teddy bears. It was the type of wallpaper that would have made Warren gag in his old, real life, Cody mused as he stepped into the barely furnished room with his mother. A nurse, who was required to stay during all visits, sat in the corner.

All that was in the room was a bed, a dresser with baby-proof latches, and Warren, crouched in his bed, staring at

The author describes the smells of the hospital and the music pumped into the air. What other sounds and smells would you hear in the Harmony Home for Children?

disinfectant: a substance that destroys germs

the wall across from him. He cowered as if there were a monster across the room, but there was nothing there but the same balloons and teddy bears that had invaded the hall.

The nurse smiled, as if it were her job to smile. "Stimulation is important for Warren," she said. "He needs to know that people still remember him—that his old life is still out there when he's ready to go back to it."

Cody cleared his throat and held on to his mother like a small child. "What's up, Warren?" he asked.

But Warren didn't turn to look at him. Instead he just hummed to himself.

Cody tentatively let go of the death-grip he had on his mother's arm and took a few steps closer.

———

"Don't let them get you!" he shrieked,

his voice a wild warble. "Stay awake all

night! Run when you see them coming!

Don't let them take you to that place."

———

Warren still didn't look at him, but he did speak.

"They let you in here?" he asked. "Why did they let you in here?"

Warren's voice sounded empty and far away. Cody noticed that his hair wasn't quite white but ashen gray, standing on end, and hopelessly tangled. This was not the Warren Burke that Cody knew.

"Yeah, sure, they let me in," Cody said, offering a lopsided smile. "You doin' okay?"

stimulation: something to stir up or excite someone

Warren shook his head and backed farther into the corner of his bed as Cody approached. "Don't let them get you!" he shrieked, his voice a wild warble. "Stay awake all night! Run when you see them coming! Don't let them take you to that place."

Cody could feel his own hair start to stand on end, but he had to ask. "Who? Who's going to get me? And where am I supposed to keep them from taking me?"

Warren could only stare at Cody in horror.

The nurse, who didn't seem pleased with the direction of the conversation, pulled open the curtains. "Maybe we could all take a look at the view," she said. And then she turned to Warren. "Why don't you tell your little friend all about the walks we've been taking around the lake, Warren? Tell him how they help your nerves."

Cody looked out the window. The view might have been beautiful elsewhere, but not for the people here. The bars on the window could never let them forget where they were.

But Warren didn't seem interested in the view anyway. He just kept staring over at the wall as if waiting for something to happen.

Suddenly Cody's mother, who had been sitting quietly by the door, turned to the nurse and asked, "Is Warren getting any . . . better?"

"Oh, yes!" chimed the nurse, as if it were her job to chime. "He's growing stronger every day!"

"Growing!" said Warren, with a sneer in his voice. Then he snapped his eyes to Cody. "You're lucky," he said. "You're lucky you're so small. Growing as fast as I did was the worst thing that ever happened to me!"

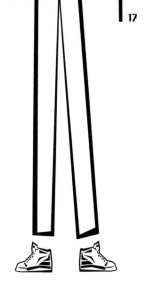

"Now, Warren," said the nurse in her practiced, soothing voice. "Remember, we have to think positive thoughts." And she cast her eyes down to the little paper cup on the dresser to make sure he had taken his medication.

"I'll never have a positive thought again," said Warren. "Not after what I saw—not after what I *felt*."

Cody couldn't resist. "What did you feel?" he asked.

Warren's eyes went wide and his lips stretched back in a grimace, as if he were feeling it all over again.

"*Growing pains,*" he hissed.

The nurse was beginning to act a little nervous. "Warren, why don't you take your little friend out to the rec room," she suggested. "You could play Ping-Pong or a nice game of Scrabble."

But Warren wasn't interested in games. He reached out, grabbed Cody by the shirt, and pulled him close.

"*We grow when we sleep . . .*" Warren whispered desperately in Cody's ear. And then, out of nowhere, he began to scream the way he had that first night—emptying his lungs, then gasping for air, and emptying his lungs over and over again.

Cody turned and ran, bursting out the door and racing down the long hallway. He didn't stop until he was outside, where Warren's screams blended in with the screams of all the other children who had gone mad.

※ ※ ※

A few days later, with the memory of the hospital still fresh in his mind, Cody visited the auto shop where his father worked. It was a restless place, where exhausted

PREDICT

What do Warren's warnings mean? What is he trying to tell Cody? What details make you think this?

mechanics created automotive wonders. There were engines torn apart into a thousand small greasy pieces that would somehow fit together like a jigsaw puzzle. There were whole cars gutted to make room for bigger engines than nature ever intended. But strangest of all was the department his father managed, where they took big Cadillacs and made them even bigger.

As Cody stepped into the shop, his father was supervising one such procedure. A blue sedan, already stripped of its doors, was practically being sawed in half because the owner wanted five more feet of legroom. But today Cody hadn't come to watch them build a limo. He had come to talk to his dad.

"Did you ever know anyone who . . . uh, snapped . . . the way Warren did?" Cody asked when he had finally gotten his father alone in his small office.

———

"I had this friend once, when I was about your age. Anyway, he went nuts, kind of the way Warren did. I wasn't there, but I heard about it—*everyone* heard about it, and there were lots of rumors."

———

"No," his father replied, but he had hesitated long enough for Cody to know that he was lying. His dad walked over and closed the door of his office, muffling the noise of the shop. Then he looked Cody straight in the eyes.

"Don't tell your mother I told you this," he said, "or she'll blame me for giving you nightmares." He cleared his throat and began to pace. "I had this friend once, when I was about your age. Anyway, he went nuts, kind of the way Warren did. I wasn't there, but I heard about it—*everyone* heard about it, and there were lots of rumors."

He paused for a moment, then went on. "Some people said my friend got hit in the head too hard—his dad was a mean son-of-a-gun. Others said he was never right in the head to begin with. Anyway, the story his parents gave was that he woke up screaming in the middle of the night, saying that the angels had come to take him. He kept on screaming, so they sent him away, and no one ever heard from him again."

"What do you think happened to your friend that night, Dad?" Cody asked.

His father scratched his neck and shrugged. "Probably nothing," he said. "And as for the things he said—well, it was just something made up by a mind that was about to go crazy . . . or already had."

Cody squirmed and felt his skin begin to crawl. "Maybe what happened to your friend is what happened to Warren," he suggested. "You see, after I ran out of Warren's room at the hospital, I sat out there on the porch of that Harmony Home place where they're keeping him, and I heard other kids screaming, too. I couldn't tell for sure, but they all seemed to be screaming about something that came in the middle of the night to take them away. Angels . . . monsters . . . aliens . . . whatever."

Cody's dad looked at him for a moment, and then laughed, slapping him on the back. "You sure have some imagination," he said. "Not bad for a little guy."

Cody gave him a cold stare. "I'm not so little."

"Oh, don't be so sensitive," said his dad. "You'll grow soon—I can feel it in my bones."

✳ ✳ ✳

They came at three in the morning.

It had been another sleepless night for Cody. He had counted about a thousand sheep and still hadn't so much as drifted off. He was about to start counting a new, larger flock of sheep . . . when they came. It began as a breeze he felt on the tip of his nose—but he remembered that his window was closed. Cody snapped his eyes open and looked across to the opposite wall.

A line had appeared—a thin black line—and it ran from ceiling to floor, spreading like a <u>fissure</u> or some kind of hole in space. Then, hands started to reach out of the hole—dozens of hands. And then, suddenly, there were people in the room! Cody tried to scream, but one large, heavy hand, cold and <u>antiseptic</u> smelling, covered his mouth. Then several others grabbed Cody's arms and legs. He struggled wildly, but the hands were strong, and with little effort, they dragged him toward the hole, drawing him through the cold, dark fissure and into a bright white light.

All at once Cody felt himself being lifted onto something . . . then he was rolling, flat on his back, and suddenly he knew he was in . . . a hospital.

PREDICT

Who or what came at three in the morning? What details make you think this?

fissure: a narrow crack that is long and deep

antiseptic: a substance that prevents infection

He was strapped down to a <u>gurney</u> and being rolled through clean white hallways. He kept his eyes fixed on a man with a clipboard, running alongside him. The man was clean-cut, clean-shaven, and had spotless white teeth.

"I'm Farnsworth, public relations," said the man with a perfect smile. "It's good to see you again, Cody. It's been a while."

"I've never seen you before!" wailed Cody, fighting to get free from the tight bonds around him.

"Of course you have," said Farnsworth reassuringly. "You just don't remember."

"Take me back home!"

"In time, Cody."

The four hospital workers who had pulled him out of bed and through the hole in space now wheeled him down the impossibly long hallway like <u>pallbearers</u> with a casket. Farnsworth jogged alongside, making sure that everything went smoothly.

"Are you . . . an angel?" asked Cody.

Farnsworth laughed. "Heavens, no," he said. "None of us are. We're just the medical staff."

Farnsworth looked at his clipboard. "Things have been busy around here lately," he said. "We're backed up—almost a year behind—and you're way overdue."

"F-for what?" Cody stammered.

"A growth spurt, of course," answered Farnsworth.

They pushed Cody through a set of double doors and into a huge room that seemed to be the size of a stadium.

"Welcome to the Growth Ward!" Farnsworth announced.

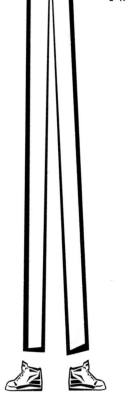

gurney: a cart with wheels, used to move patients around in hospitals

pallbearers: people who walk with the coffin at a funeral

In the room were thousands of surgeons, huddled together over patients . . . all of whom were kids.

Cody couldn't believe what he was seeing. It was like his father's auto shop, but instead of cars it was kids being taken apart and put back together again—piece by piece. But what was most amazing of all was that these kids, in various stages of repair, were all alive!

And they were also awake.

Some screamed, others just groaned, and the ones who no longer had the strength to even groan just watched in terror as the "medical staff" dismantled them, then rebuilt them before their own horrified eyes.

"What are you doing to them?" shouted Cody. "What's going on here?"

"Body work and scheduled maintenance, of course," said Farnsworth over the awful wails around him. "How can people be expected to grow without their maintenance appointments?"

"You're killing them!" yelled Cody.

"Nonsense, our surgeons are the most skilled in the universe," said Farnsworth cheerfully. "These kids will be patched up and back to their old selves by morning—and without a single scar from the experience."

"But I don't need surgery. I don't WANT surgery," Cody insisted.

"Why should you be different from everyone else?" asked Farnsworth. "And besides, you *do* want it." He smiled. "You do want to grow, don't you?"

Cody felt weak and sick to his stomach. "You mean . . . *this* happens to everybody?"

"Of course it does," explained Farnsworth. "Nobody remembers, though, because we erase it from their memory." Then the smile left Farnsworth's face, and he shook his head sadly. "Of course, every once in a while the memory erasing doesn't quite work. It's a shame, really—those poor kids are ruined for life, and all because they couldn't forget the Growth Ward."

Cody was still trying to digest what Farnsworth had just said, when he was rolled into a bright area where a group of surgeons waited. Their faces covered with masks, they anxiously flexed their fingers like pianists preparing for a concert. As Cody stared in horror at them, he noticed that there was something about those surgeons—something not quite right, but what was it? Keeping his eyes glued on them, Cody knew if he looked at them long enough, he'd figure out what it was that made them look . . . different.

PREDICT

What do you think will happen to Cody in the Growth Ward? Why do you think as you do?

As Cody stared in horror at them, he noticed that there was something about those surgeons—something not quite right, but what was it?

"It says here, we're adding half an inch to your forearms today," Farnsworth said, glancing at his clipboard again. "And a whole inch to your thigh bones. Good for you, Cody! We'll have you caught up to those other kids in your class in no time!"

Cody turned to see a silver tray next to the operating table. On it were a few small, circular bone fragments, no larger than Lego pieces.

One of the eager surgeons grabbed a small bone saw from the tray and turned it on. It buzzed and whined, adding to the many unpleasant sounds of the great galactic operating room.

The surgeon said nothing and moved the saw toward Cody's leg, and the others approached him with their scalpels poised.

"No!" Cody cried. "You can't operate without anesthesia! I have to have an anesthetic!"

Farnsworth chuckled. "Come now, Cody, where do you think you are, at the dentist? I think not! Growing pains are a part of life, and *everyone* has to feel their growing pains. *Everyone.*"

Cody screamed even before the instruments touched his body—then he suddenly realized that it didn't matter how loud he wailed. For he had finally figured out what was wrong with those surgeons. They couldn't hear him. They had no ears.

✳ ✳ ✳

I need to remember . . .
I need to remember . . .
I need to remember . . . what?

An alarm tore Cody out of the deepest sleep he had ever had. There was a memory of a dream—or something like a dream—but it was quickly fading into darkness. In a

You've had growing pains, haven't you? Based on your own experiences, add one or two more details to this description of the operating room.

galactic: huge

scalpels: small, straight knives used by doctors in surgery

anesthesia: loss of the feeling of pain, produced by ether or some other drug

moment it was completely gone, and all that was left was the light of day pouring into his room.

"Wake up, lazy bones," said his mother. "You'll be late for school."

Cody felt good this morning. No—*better* than good—he felt great, and he couldn't quite tell why. He stood up out of bed and felt a slight sensation of <u>vertigo</u>, as if the floor were somehow farther away from him than it had been the day before. His legs and arms ached the slightest bit, but that was okay. It was a *good* feeling.

"My, how you're growing!" his mother said as he walked into the kitchen for breakfast. "I'll bet you'll grow three inches by fall!"

And the thought made Cody smile. It felt good to be a growing boy.

vertigo: dizziness, often caused by a fear of heights

Tiny Terror

Some models are so authentic, it's hard to believe they're not real.

This was Craig's best model yet. He'd spent countless hours getting every little detail just right. This one was special. It was a model helicopter. Craig had gone through ships and tanks and cars, but he had finally decided that he liked putting together war planes the most. This was an Apache attack chopper, and even Craig couldn't believe how authentic it looked, like a real Apache had been shrunk to fit in his hand.

It took him a lot of practice to get his models to look this good. He learned how to use steel wool to scratch away paint so they looked like they were really used. He even learned how to use a fine paintbrush to paint the figures of the pilots so every detail of their uniforms and their faces stood out.

As Craig set the chopper pilot down, he thought he wouldn't be surprised if the figure picked up its tiny flight gear, walked across to its helicopter, and climbed inside. But when the miniature pilot did just that, Craig wasn't just surprised, he was shocked. He watched in disbelief as the pilot leaned over and conferred with his copilot. The two of them looked at Craig, then at each other, and nodded. They started the engine, and the tiny chopper lifted off from Craig's desk, took a lazy turn around the room, and then started speeding toward Craig. Terrified, he dived under his desk as the tiny guns he had painstakingly painted <u>barraged</u> him with miniature bullets that actually made dents all over his desk.

———

The little pilots were smiling

as the helicopter followed him around

the room. Craig knew it was only a

matter of time before they fired one of

the heat-seeking missiles at him.

Then it would all be over.

———

The helicopter <u>hovered</u> above the desk. Craig watched as the two pilots discussed their next move—then, without warning, the chopper flew directly toward him, machine guns blazing. The tiny bullets stung, and Craig blinked back tears as he leaped out from under the desk.

The little pilots were smiling as the helicopter followed him around the room. Craig knew it was only a matter of time before they fired one of the heat-seeking missiles at him. Then it would all be over. Craig desperately looked around the room for something he could use as a weapon to fight back. But his mom had just made him clean his room—no baseball bat or tennis racket was within range.

barraged: shot a stream of artillery fire

hovered: stayed in one place in the air

Then he saw his weapon. He made a mad dash back to his modeling bench. The tiny pilot and his crew tried to cut him off. They fired one of the heat-seeking missiles, and Craig barely had time to put his hand up before it blew up in his palm. He cried out in pain, but he didn't have time to look at the damage. He grabbed the can of spray paint on the bench and spun toward the attacking chopper, spraying a blinding coat of paint over the windshield. The pilots' panic-stricken faces appeared out of the side windows for just a second. Then the chopper, flying blindly out of control, <u>veered</u> wildly around the room before crashing into a wall. Craig stood over the burning wreckage and watched as the pilot and copilot tried to crawl out. Then, with one swift stamp of his foot, he coldly crushed the tiny men beneath his sneaker.

Craig breathed a sigh of relief. It was over, he thought—until he heard a sound from his shelf. With rising dread, Craig stared at the rest of the war planes— the ones he'd built with such deadly accuracy. Slowly, surely, each plane was aiming its perfect miniature guns directly at his heart.

veered: changed direction

GROWING PAINS

▼ Learning from the Story

Both "Growing Pains" and "Tiny Terror" are interesting stories. But if you were going to tape either of them, you'd definitely want to add sound effects. Working with several other students, select a page or two from one of the stories. Decide what sound effects you'd like to add. Work together to figure out how to create these sounds. Then have one student act as narrator and others take the parts of the different characters, while the rest of you add sound effects at the appropriate times.

▼ Putting It into Practice

Some stories sound great on paper, but they lose something when you read them aloud. The sentences may be too long. The action could be hard to follow.

Read through your own nightmarish story. As you read, insert ideas for sound effects that would help establish your setting or add to the mood and suspense. Work with a partner to create these sounds. You may be able to record some of these sound effects from movies and CDs about similar subjects.

I Know What You're Doing

Did you ever have that creepy feeling that you're being watched?

I know who you are. I know where you live. In fact, I'm watching you this very minute.

You don't believe me?

Well, I can prove it to you. I know what you're doing right now, right this very second. In fact, I'll tell you.

You're reading the last story in this book.

You think that's funny? You think it's a joke?

It's not. I'm serious. Dead serious.

I know everything about you. I knew you would get this book. Oh, I didn't know if you'd buy it yourself or if somebody would buy it for you. I wasn't sure if you'd pick it up at a bookstore or get it through a book club or at school—or even if you'd find it at a friend's house. I didn't know how you'd get hold of it. I just knew that, eventually, this book would arrive in the hands of the person it was intended for . . . *you.*

Right about now you might be wondering who *I* am.

No, don't bother looking at the table of contents. That isn't me. The authors of the rest of these stories—well, let's just say I took care of them. I ripped them apart with my claws. The police thought they were killed by a wild animal—maybe you read about it? Probably not. I mean, it's not like they were R. L. Stine or Stephen King or anything. Their deaths weren't important enough to make the papers.

They had finished thirteen stories when I killed them. Then I sent the fourteenth story—*this* story, the one you're reading—to their bublisher.

(Sorry, I meant "publisher." It's so hard to type with these claws. It was so much easier when I used to be in human form.)

Anyway, their editor didn't know the difference, and the book was published. All I had to do was wait for you to get it.

I was watching when you picked it up for the first time. I saw you look at the cover, open the book, then start scanning it. I studied the expression on your face. I've been watching you ever since, waiting for you to reach *this* story.

You still don't believe me? You really don't think that I'm watching you right now. You think I'm making all this up.

Well, I can prove it to you . . . and I will, in less than a minute.

So maybe you're wondering why I'm doing this to you. Well, maybe I have a reason, and maybe I don't. Maybe I'll tell you, and maybe I won't . . . when I see you . . . *tonight*.

Remember? I know where you live. I know where your bedroom is. I know—

Oh, yes . . . I said I'd prove to you that I was watching you. Well, I'll prove it to you right now . . .

You just turned the page, didn't you? Yes, you did—you can't deny it! How else would you be reading this?

Anyway, don't worry. You won't know when I'll come for you, and you won't feel a thing . . . I'll just wait until you fall asleep. And then . . .

I Know What You're Doing

▼ Learning from the Story

This story has an intriguing plot. It plays on your own fears. It has a main character that you can really relate to—you! It is told from a first-person point of view and written from a unique perspective. The setting is wherever you are. This story has everything—except an ending!

In a small group, discuss how the author paints pictures in your mind and creates a terrifying mood. Then write a paragraph or two to finish the story.

▼ Putting It into Practice

Read over your own nightmare story and get ready to record it.

- Underline words you want to emphasize.
- Make notes to yourself about where you should pause and where you will add sound effects.
- Read your story aloud several times, to yourself or to anyone who will listen, until you get it just right.
- Coordinate your music and sound effects with your reading.

Now you're ready to record your story!